Eclectic Rambling

Extended

John B. Leber

Copyright © 2012 John B. Leber

ISBN:061561499X
ISBN-13:978-0-615-61499-1

DEDICATION

Dedicated to my folks, who never let me know what I "couldn't" do.

And to Bill.

John B. Leber

Eclectic Rambling

Eclectic Rambling is exactly that. It is about plucking the pearls of wisdom and intriguing images from an interesting sixty odd years of life. If this is anything, it should be fun. No pedantic pandering philosophy or mental meandering here. There are, of course, elements of high drama and low humor, but life is like that; at least mine has been.

Looking about my small home office, I see my two college degrees. One, from Carleton College in Northfield, Minnesota, I cannot read because it's in Latin. It's a Bachelor of Art, no less. The other, in English, is a B. S. O. E. or a Bachelor of Science in Ocean Engineering. That one I can read, more or less. It's written in English, but with words like "thereunto," if that is, in fact, a word.

Looking about sixty odd years of life, I feel fortunate. I have seen the North Atlantic in all her fury and the sun rising behind Sugarloaf Mountain in Rio de Janeiro. And I still have most of my teeth and some of my hair!

Ok, I promised pearls of wisdom and intriguing images. Here we go.

What the heck does one do with an Ocean Engineering degree anyway? Well, in my case, I went to work in very early 1981 for a company called Sedco Inc., then the premier harsh environment offshore drilling company. I spent years working on a rig called the Sedco 706 located at that time about 300 miles off St. John's, Newfoundland, and consider those years among the best years that I've had. While more than 30 years ago now, some memories are as clear now as they were the day after.

On Running Anchors

It's a gray evening, with blackness surrounding the couple of hundred feet of dimly lit ocean and misty air. It's two in the morning, and everyone looks forward to finishing. 4 anchors are out, with 4 to go. This time it's #2 and #6, sitting on opposite corners of the rig. Mine is six, sitting on the port after corner. My supply boat sits quietly, 50 feet off the port side, amidships. The ocean is friendly tonight, with long, slow ten foot swells gently rocking all, belying the wild ride to come.

The port crane fires up with a great puff of black smoke, its diesel engine noisy and strong. The roustabouts, keeping a constant vigil on the always moving headache ball, wait patiently as the crane booms down and rotates to reach the anchor pennant. My winch shack, cantilevered out over the ocean, vibrates slightly in sync with the crane's diesel.

On marine channel 6, I listen as the First Mate chats with the crane op, discussing his latest exploits shore side. The crane operator, a jovial fellow from Nova Scotia, suggests that there might be embellishment, and the banter continues until the roustabouts have slung the pennant on the ball hook.

The crane winches up, and the heavy three inch diameter steel wire pennant is lifted off the hanger. Swinging, booming down, and winching down all at once, the crane op drops the pennant eye to the supply boat deck. With the practiced ease of experienced deck hands, the pennant eye is secured to the boats winch, and the crane un-slung. As the crane winches and swings clear, the boat's winch slowly wraps up the pennant until the anchor, a million pound rating, is pulled up and onto the after deck, the steel three inch diameter pennant collar rolling smoothly on the ten foot diameter roller at the aft of the boats deck. The misty air reverberates as the anchor climbs up and falls to the deck, trailing chain over the roller and into the sea.

I look at the chart on the winch shack wall, with a chart of distance out across the top, water depth on the left edge, and anchor tension in each box. Our water depth is a fairly shallow 300 feet, so I will follow that row on the chart. The goal is to get the anchor as far out as possible.

The anchor and chain are rated at a million pounds. The chain weighs one hundred pounds per foot. The chain comes out of a chain locker in the column beneath me, over the windlass right behind me (as big as a one car garage), and down the column's exterior through a fairleader (a thing like a pulley wheel mounted on the column) well below water line. My method of control is a huge band brake, cooled by running water.

It's quiet as the two supply boats on opposite corners of the rig jockey themselves into position. I take the mechanical brake off, keeping enough tension with the band brake that the chain cannot just pile up the ocean floor. Most of the roustabouts have gone into quarters for a smoke. The only noise is the water pouring over the band brake. The two boat captains agree to start.

For just a second I can hear the roar of the boat's engines as her stern drops and she turns the ocean behind her into white fury. Then the chain starts running out, banging and clanking with such noise that I can hear nothing else as my little winch shack vibrates up and down so much my glasses stay on only because they have an elastic strap around my head. Even though I can hear nothing from the radio, I announce footage "#6-200". 150 feet below me, a ballast tank is being flooded at maximum speed to compensate for the loss in weight of the chain.

The chart tells me to increase tension, to hold the outgoing chain off the ocean floor. My shack is now vibrating so much I can read the chart only with difficulty. As the tension increases, the water pouring over the band brakes turns to mist, billowing around the windlass and drifting through my little shack. The mist hits my glasses and condenses.

The world has shrunk to my shack and my task. The noise almost prohibits thought. My entire focus is on three things, the chart, which I glance at occasionally to check, the footage counter, and the tension gauge. The band brake pad begins to smoke and char, and the air begins to smell of running anchors. The smoke sticks to my glasses and my face. "#6-2000" I say into the void.

Almost as quickly as it starts, it's over. Final outage, 4500, a very good run, and we beat #2 by 200 feet. The shack is still, and quickly the hissing of the water running over the band brake turns to the noise of running water again. I can both hear and think. The supply boat notifies me that the anchor is down. I clean my glasses and notify the boat that I am tensioning, and hear the huge electric motor in the windlass whine as I slowly tension the chain up to tension spec.

That done, I notify the boat that I am slacking off to operating spec. I am done. The boat will drag the anchor pennant back down the chain to the rig, and the crane will pick it up and hang it off. I cannot wait to get to the coffee shack for coffee, to get the taste and smell of running anchors out of my mouth and nose. Total time spent....maybe 5 minutes.

It's a gray evening, with blackness surrounding the couple of hundred feet of dimly lit ocean and misty air. It's three in the morning, and everyone looks forward to finishing. 6 anchors are out, with 2 to go.

The Leaf

I have taken thousands of photographs, but without question, the best is one I call "The Leaf". I was on the blacktop parking lot of a post office, on a gray day with a soft rain. Apparently, a car had leaked some gas, and it had spread out on top of the rain water, a rainbow of soft colors. Towards the center of the spill was a small maple leaf.

Soft blues and purples ripple across both the leaf and the different small pebbles embedded in the black top. It is truly beautiful. It is not, as it has been called, a "powerful anti-pollution statement." It is simply a bit of nature's beauty captured on film. Oops, I feel a digression coming...

I just called a gasoline spill on a blacktop parking lot a bit of nature's beauty. I have no doubt that will raise some hackles for some of you (assuming this book is ever published and there ever are "some of you").

Ok, in defense of that statement, in the first place, I am writing this, and for me a gasoline spill on a black top parking lot can be some of nature's beauty! However, since you're taking the time to read this, I will explain the reasoning.

It has always struck me as supreme arrogance to separate man from nature, as though there were nature on the one hand (everything but mankind), and mankind on the other. That false separation can also really muddy our thinking about environmental issues. In a very real sense, nature will be fine no matter what we do. However, it is a very, very different issue whether or not nature will be to our liking as a result of what we do.

There are colonies of sub-sea worm things that live in one area until that area is so fouled with their waste that they cannot live there any longer. Lots of species go through explosive growth and massive death cycles. Lots of species impact other species very, very heavily.

It always seemed to me, thinking of Darwin's theory of evolution, that there are secondary (and probably tertiary and more) levels of competition, not just a competition between species. It seems to me that ecosystems compete with ecosystems. The prairie competes with the forest. Grasslands compete with wetlands.

Looking at it that way, farmland also competes with prairie, with the farmer simply one specie who is quite successful at manipulating his environment, not unlike beavers who build dams to alter theirs or termites who build towers to control theirs.

There is no intended religious connotation here at all, merely comments on an environmental model. The perspective I prefer removes a "right" and "wrong" aspect to environmental concerns. If we pollute this planet so badly that there is nothing left but brown sludge and bacteria, nature will be fine. At that point, nature will consist of brown sludge and bacteria. We, of course, would have become part of the brown sludge.

Personally, I would prefer not to be part of the brown sludge. For me, all environmental issues boil down to a single question: will this action move me or my descendants closer to or further away from becoming brown sludge? The beauty of phrasing the issue that way is that it removes "holier than thou" arguments. It also leaves open almost infinite avenues for argument.

For example, I really don't care about Spotted Owls (So shoot me...I just plain don't care). However, I also don't know very much about what function they serve in an environment which I like. That admission opens room for debate, but debate on issues and fact, not the sanctity of Spotted Owls.

Heavens, where was I? Oh yes, photography. "The Leaf" is the kind of photography I love to do at its best. I love to find the exquisite beauty which few folks bother to see. It's all around us, all of the time. All of nature has its own beauty, whether it's the Grand Tetons or a junk yard in Chicago. For me, anyway, it is arrogant to say that one beauty is "better" than another, and a reflection of a tendency we all have to replace logic and information with value judgments.

Wow, from photography to soapbox to photography to soapbox, all in one chapter! I must be on a roll tonight, I should quit while I'm a head (said the lettuce----sorry).

Homeward from Spokane

I think it was 1996 (late breaking correction from Liz, my virtual sister—it was 1997) when I drove to Spokane, WA, to meet a lady I had gotten to know on AOL, which is another story. My mother-in-law was coming to visit my separated wife between Christmas and New Year's, and since she was so seldom able to be here, it just made sense for the kids to stay with my wife, who was living in a small town west of Peoria.

Mostly, I didn't want to be in town, so, once again, I headed west, this time in a 1989 Buick Century. After the visit (as I said...another story) it was late afternoon on New Year's Day when I left Spokane headed for Peoria. The departure, in part, was precipitated by an oncoming winter storm. Once in a while there are windows of time where the regular rules don't seem to apply, and this night certainly ended up being one of those times.

I think it was around 9 in the evening when the storm caught up with me at the top of a pass in eastern Washington. Suddenly, light rain, then light snow, then snow so heavy you had to guess where the road was by the tree lines and the posts every so often along the shoulder. Even 10 miles an hour was pushing it.

Over the top, and within 10 or 15 minutes, the road was dry, the air clear. It was then I noticed the western half of the sky was pitch black. The eastern half had stars. So the race was on!

Three times the storm caught me, always briefly, always at the top of a pass. In between, I drove the road like it was a video game. I don't really know how fast I went. I know I used both lanes and sometimes both shoulders to soften the curves. I never saw traffic going my way, and only very, very seldom saw traffic going west (you would have had to REALLY want to go west to be going west right then).

I stopped for gas (far western Montana, I think) and walked into the station to refill my thermos in pleasant conditions, light wind, no rain or snow at all. By the time I walked out, there was driving rain and wind so strong that signs were blowing over. It was a spectacular storm!

In about ten minutes I was ahead of the rain. My car was a cocoon. Three constant noises kept me company, tires drumming on

7

pavement, wind on the windows, and the comforting sounds of a smooth running engine. The dash lights were enough to see my thermos and coffee cup.

There were no elk to be seen. I think they must have known what was chasing me, and were hunkered down in the deepest thickets they could find. The world was just the storm and I, racing each other across far western Montana.

There is something very satisfying about a reality which totally consumes you. No worries, no time to worry. Watching the lay of the land, trying to out guess the wind. Glancing at the sky, gauging how far ahead you are. In the "in between" times, a straight stretch of road or a long gentle curve, reflecting on other times. Remembering the cowboy at the rest stop, and how spectacular this country is. I felt like the road was mine, the storm was mine, the time was mine.

The time was mine, and I still treasure it.

On Ted and sky diving

While we are all special, a few individuals, for whatever reason, leave a huge and lasting impression on us. We need to treasure and reflect on both those individuals and the reasons why they have come to mean so much to us. In this way, I think, we can improve ourselves and our lives.

Before I became an engineer, I lived in S. Florida, on the Gold Coast, for a few years. How and why are other stories, but it was a colorful time, and full of colorful people.

To this day I think of Ted as a "force of nature." He befriended me when I was boat sitting a 73 foot long 50 year old Lawley motor yacht named Tropic in Hypoluxo, Florida. When he wanted to, he could charm absolutely anyone. Although I never saw it, I am also sure that when he wanted to, he could terrify anyone.

He had the bluest eyes I have ever seen, and a knife scar down one cheek to his chin. His was the body of a boxer, which he had been, Golden Gloves in the Army, I think. His code of life was simple, anything for your friends (absolutely anything), and anything (absolutely anything) to your enemies. If I had known who and what he was when we first met, I would have been too terrified to talk to him.

He befriended me because I had charge of Tropic, the biggest, nicest yacht in Hypoluxo Marina, where he had Irma. Irma was his sailboat, a gaff rigged double ender which sailed like a pig. She was a converted lifeboat, wood over steel. Eventually, he married Sandy on Tropic, and I was the wedding photographer.

It was at that wedding that I met Judi, the first great love of my life. Judi's brother, a real scuzbag, was Sandy's ex-husband. Judi and Sandy had become friends while cruising sordid little bars in south Florida trying to find him. South Florida has an abundance of sordid little bars! But those are all other stories.

Ted decided that he, another boat owner named Dusty, and I should go sky diving. He knew of a place run by a man named Poppenhager where you could take a four hour class and then go up and jump out of a plane. No piggybacking with a trained instructor, no static line, just jump and free fall.

Rumor had it that the authorities couldn't force Poppenhager to require five static line jumps before a free fall. According to general scuttlebutt this was because Poppenhager had secretly trained the jumpers for the Bay of Pigs invasion, so the authorities couldn't force Poppenhager to do anything he didn't want to do. Of course, south Florida loves rumors.

I never knew Dusty very well. He had an old wooden sailboat at the marina which had a quartz window in the hull well below waterline. He had been a medic in Vietnam, and left the marina shortly after our jump to find the underwater road someone claimed to have found in the Bahamas and follow it to Atlantis. At that time, Hypoluxo Marina was the cheapest birthing on south Florida's east coast, so lots of interesting folks floated in and out.

The day arrived, and sure enough, we took a short course, learning to jump and roll off of a four foot high platform, learning to count to 5, learning to assume the landing position at 300 feet, and learning to read the altimeter so we would know when 300 feet came around. That last point was apparently critical. The instructor left no doubt that if you did not turn your chute into the wind, bend your knees, and assume the landing position at 300 feet, and survived anyway, he would kill you.

We learned that the harness you wear has four risers, thick straps really, two on each shoulder, which connect to the many shrouds, smaller lines, which lead up to the parachute. We learned that if anything looked awry, to pull the emergency chute. We learned that you can "dump" the air in a parachute, effectively turning it into a large rag. By the end of the course, we knew the terminology and a multitude of potential problems I had never considered. They also stressed "keeping the arch", referring to the proper position for free fall.

Then we chuted up and climbed into a small Cessna. Our helmets had a small radio built in, so an advisor on the ground could talk to us if he felt the need. The pilot was drinking something from a can hidden by a foam insulator, and wearing a round golf hat with pop tops (that was back when beer can pop tops popped off) ringing it like Christmas ornaments. As we taxied out, we passed the burned out remnants of a small plane. It was only later that I guessed it was a plot to help first time jumpers jump. In my case, it worked. By the time we took off, I figured it was safer to jump back to earth than to land in the plane.

I don't remember if I was 2nd or 3rd, I only know I was not first. The amazing thing is that when someone jumps out of a small plane, to those who remain, they are gone, as if they had never been there. Just totally, absolutely, gone, like a few of my old girlfriends.

When my turn came, I did as I was supposed to do, and held the wing strut as I stepped onto the wheel cover. Only then did it sink in that I was actually going to do this! Then, I stepped off.

I believe human beings stop accelerating at about 140 miles per hour. The wind noise was deafening. I started to feel like I was tumbling and snapped to a better arch, and felt myself stabilize.

Unknown to me, a group of a about 10 very experienced jumpers jumped together from another plane, far higher and upwind from me. I found out later that my ground advisor lost track of me with so many in his line of sight. I think this ended up being a blessing.

Anyway, as I stabilized with a better arch, I had a momentary feeling of pride of accomplishment. And then it struck me. I had not been counting! And geez, we had practiced counting. The instructors had been rigorous about that. No student could jump until they knew, for certain, how to count to at least 5!

The ripcord was over my right chest. I decided, in the absence of counting, that it would behoove me to assume 5. Now, in class, they never really went into detail on the mechanics of pulling the ripcord. Either that, or I wasn't paying attention to that part. There were, periodically, lovely ladies passing through, often in what south Florida calls summer attire, and I will admit that my attention wavered once in a while.

Anyway, the right way to pull the ripcord is to use the right hand, carefully keeping the arch, and snap the hand in, and pull the ripcord with the same motion that returns the hand back to its free fall position. I, however, was going to pull that ripcord no matter how hard it was to pull, and used both hands, shoulders hunching to gain power. That, of course, broke the arch.

The chute opened, the wind noise stopped, and I think this is when I opened my eyes, or at least began paying attention to sight again. I am not too proud to say that I am generally a very observant person. In absolutely no time at all, I deduced that I was hanging upside down. Further, it did not require my superb training in science and analytical thinking to figure out that while there was no discomfort at all in drifting back to earth upside down, that would certainly not be true of arrival.

I also remember the thought, "Ok John. It's up to you", which was in a strange way comforting. It was certainly a situation where any physical assistance from anyone else was an impossibility. Fortunately for me, the problem at hand was sufficiently pressing that I didn't even feel afraid. I also think it was fortunate for me that I did not have the voice of some guy standing safely on the ground telling me to "not panic."

Examining my situation, I found I was hanging by my left leg. The two left risers were twisted around each other one way, then my leg stuck between, and then they untwisted and went up to the shrouds. My chute, which should have been a circle, was an oval, which meant that I was without a doubt descending faster than I was supposed to be.

I think my altitude at this point was 2000 feet. I could pull the emergency chute, strapped on my stomach, but they tell you in class that if you do that, to be very careful not to get tangled in it. With a much lower air speed, the emergency chute will billow and float around you until it fully opens. I decided to wait until 1000 feet, and if still tangled up, pull the emergency. That way, if it wrapped around my neck, I might reach the ground before strangling (at least if I were hanging by the neck, I would be right side up---I guess life really is all about trade-offs).

So, I did a hand over hand climb up my left leg to pull down enough slack to free my leg. Now that was scary! If I pulled down too much, and dumped the chute, I would be falling, dragging a large rag behind. But that large rag would be enough resistance to ensure that I still landed on my head!

Well, I didn't dump the chute, and I did extricate my leg. The chute fully opened, I jerked to a slower speed, and it was really cool, for about 30 seconds. Then I looked down, which was finally under my feet instead of my head. Because I had been descending far faster than I should have been, I was way off the target landing spot. In fact, I was coming down in the airport parking area, fortunately grass, but with parked planes and power or phone lines under me.

Now, the kind of chutes that we had fly forward at 4 to 5 miles per hour, and are steered by rotating them. I found out later that there is a small lag time to get going forward after a rotation, however. So, as I rotated the chute and did not appear move off the wires under me, I rotated some more. I am fairly certain I guaranteed a spiral down to the wires.

However, I remembered my training. At 300 feet, I turned into the wind and assumed the landing position. I did not know, when my feet hit something, if it was the ground or the wires. I fell on my back and literally watched the shrouds and my chute slide along the wires as they slowly joined me on the ground.

When the chute fell to the ground, I rolled over and got to my knees. One of the young teenagers who packed the chutes was running across the grass to me and he yelled, "Are you ok?"

I yelled back "Yes!" expecting something like "oh thank God!" in return. Silly me. He immediately yelled, with all the caring sympathy of a marine drill instructor, "THEN STAND UP!"

Unknown to me, the pilot of the advanced jumpers' plane had noticed my predicament, and had been circling me during most of my descent. Feeling chastised without knowing why, I reluctantly stood up, and the world knew that I was ok, that there would be no lawyers, no newspaper articles, and no bad press.

To Ted's amazement, one week later, I went back and made my second and last jump, without incident. I believe that was when Ted decided that even though I had a college degree, even though I had never fired a firearm in anger, and even though I obeyed the law (well, the occasional traffic law excepted) that I was "ok."

I think of Ted yet today. Sometimes we are so fortunate that someone incredibly special becomes a part of our lives for a while. Ted was that for me. I never told him, but I think he knew. More on Ted later.

I wish I had told him.

Rabbit hunting and blue chairs

As much as there are lessons and images in tough times and intense times, there is joy and humor and love in family times, silly times, and the everyday oddities which make up life. We need those to leaven the other times, and should treasure their memories.

I lived with my maternal grandparents on and off, summers in high school and college, mostly. During summers they lived on a farm in southwestern Iowa, near a town called Creston, which long ago had the best chocolate malts in the world. Those were very good days.

Granddad would sit in the evening on a wooden swing and listen to baseball on the radio after dark. Sitting on the swing, we faced south, toward the barn, which sat across an expanse of mowed barnyard. The barn later left during a storm, but at the time it marked the southern boundary of the yard, beyond it was corn, or soybeans, depending on the year.

The barnyard fence ran east from the road, at the far edge of the barn. It then turned north, and ran behind the garage, on the eastern edge of the yard. It continued north past the apple orchard, where it turned west to return to the road. Beyond it to the north lay a fallow field, sloping down to the pond about a half mile away. It was a civilized fence, a wide steel mesh, not the barbed wire used for fields.

In between the swing and the barn, across the gravel driveway, was the mercury vapor barnyard light on top of a three story pole. It sat right next to a huge mulberry tree, and in the evening, its light was the measure of home. The swing, the garage, and the yard were just an extension of the house because that light made it friendly and known. Sometimes, in early summer, Granddad and I would sit and watch raccoon cubs trying to eat June bugs under the light.

June bugs are, without any doubt at all, some of God's most stupid creatures. They would fly around the light until they couldn't fly any more, and then drop to the ground, where the baby raccoons, inexperienced and total novices at hunting, could eat them at will. One summer it was skunk kits, but the scampering play was the same.

Granddad and I never talked much on the swing. He would smoke his cigar and rock the swing with a very slow, steady rhythm that creaked the chain twice a minute or so. He puffed his cigar and listened to a ballgame on the radio and watched. But in ways hard to explain, there was a connection. I was sitting on the swing with him. Watching with him. He was my grandfather, and we sat under the Iowa stars together for many a quiet evening. I still miss him yet today.

But I digress horribly. One fall I decided to test the weatherproofing claims of a spray paint manufacturer, and painted an old wooden chair a very bright blue. The grandparents packed up and went back to Peoria for the winter, and I moved into town to go to a local junior college. I left the chair standing in between the swing and the garage, a colorful blotch looking out of place as everything else turned to the grays and browns of late fall.

That winter, a friend of mine who was attending law school in New York City called me and wanted to visit. One of the things he wanted to do was experience "hunting." So it was that on a bitterly cold winter day we drove out to the farm to hunt rabbits. I loaded my single shot 12-gauge shotgun while we walked out through the gate in the fence behind the garage and headed north, into the wind. I explained, feeling very sage, that you always hunted upwind in bitter cold, so you could have your back to the wind when you were cold and headed home.

We walked and walked. Apparently all the rabbits were sensible enough to be hunkered well down in the bitter cold. There wasn't even much rabbit sign in the snow. Finally, I gave up and we headed back.

I was really disappointed. I had learned to hunt and fish in Iowa, and really wanted to share my knowledge and love of the outdoors with a friend who wanted to learn. He was a good sport about it, and we were talking and laughing as we passed the orchard, walking outside the fence.

Then a rabbit bolted just inside the fence! Apparently he had been under the snow, possibly looking for old apples that had been missed by others. He was going full bore toward the garage, and I tried to step away from my friend to have a safe shot. Well, that rabbit, going at top speed, ran right into that bright blue chair, smashed his head, and killed himself.

I was stunned. Never had I seen such a thing. My dreams of impressing my friend with my woodsman ship were shattered. When we got to the chair, the rabbit was still twitching. I paced off the distance in the snow between hops. That rabbit had been covering between six and seven feet a jump! The last foot to the chair had been a slide, to no avail.

My friend went back to the city, and I haven't seen him since. But to this day I imagine him a swank, polished big city lawyer sitting in a fine restaurant, commenting that he once saw how they hunt rabbits in southwestern Iowa. "Well, in the fall, you get a wooden chair and paint it bright blue........"

Women

I am well over 50 and to me, women are still magical, mystical, maniacal, mysterious, and majestic creatures. They are, of course, a lot of other things too, including human. I was a skinny, awkward kid, and grew up with my share of fear of women, or at least girls at that time.

I still remember how totally and absolutely horrified I was the first time I mistook a mother for a "babe." I was in high school and in a McDonalds. There was a super looking girl in a fairly tight sweater and miniskirt, waiting for food at the counter. Heck, I was a teenage boy…I looked. Her tray was ready and she paid and walked past (swish swish).

But when she reached her table, she joined two little kids who called her Mommy! I was horrified! My lord, I had been ogling a mother! Ewwww, yuk! At my age then, mothers were not women, in a sexual sense, anyway. "Mothers" probably never had sex at all. Mothers were, well, mothers.

Now, of course, I am quite comfortable with the concept of a sexy and desirable grandmother. I know a few of them, more than a few of them, actually.

For one, I am the middle aged fantasy of the "life that should have been." For another, I am just a very good friend. Melissa loved me and I sure enjoyed and valued her friendship and company. And the one my thoughts keep drifting to I helped to climb on a train to go and "make a life" with the one she loves. Life sure is strange.

Sometimes I sit in my office at night, the only lights my small banker's light on the desk and the screen, and listen to soft jazz, alone with my thoughts. The wall clock ticks, the computer fan whirs, the piano and the saxophone trade off following the melody. The piano leads the group upbeat, and the sax follows, while the drummer uses only brushes. The sax drifts into minor chords, and the piece closes, leaving much unsaid.

Times like this make me wish I could play country guitar. I could sit on my front porch bench (salvaged from the wooden wagon Grandad took us all down to the pond with), pluck a few strings, and make up a song… My dogs are gathering, I must be feeling something. They are a barometer of me. If I am sad, they hang very close.   If I am angry, they are nervous.   If I am asleep, they are protective.

Ok, I started out talking about women and digressed to dogs. What can I say?   Either "discretion is the better part of valor" or "avoidance can be a good thing", take your pick.

Perhaps a poem is in order......

You sigh and stir and I wake briefly.
Feeling you, I go back to sleep,
knowing you're with me.
With me and mine to keep.

Soft curves and gentle heart,
Quiet soul and perfect mind,
Beauty and pure form in art.
Love personified in kind.

In all my years I knew not before,
the love of one like my Labrador.

The Bahamas with Ted to get Irma

Sometimes, I think, we learn from things only years later. At least if we're honest.

Ted sometimes kept Irma at Fisherman's Cove in Bimini. One sunny day in Hypoluxo, he told me that he had enough cash to pay her back dockage and asked if I would fly over and sail her back with him. It sounded like a lot of fun, and a good adventure, so I agreed.

A day or two later we flew out of Miami on Chaucer, the sea plane service to the islands. Well, it turned out Ted didn't have quite enough cash, so he couldn't get his boat, or at least that's what he told me. In no time at all he had charmed a young Frenchman, the sole occupant and crew for a docked luxury sailing yacht. The boat actually had a bathtub!

We found ourselves sitting in the bar while Ted bought the drinks and secured an invitation for us to bunk on the yacht that night. I will admit that much of that night is none too clear in my memory, but some things are not forgotten. In retrospect, I wonder how much of that night was orchestrated by Ted on purpose.

It was well after dark and a number of drinks when two ladies joined us. One was short and plump and the other was a little taller, very shapely, with a pretty but plain face. Ted made it clear that he had bought their services for the Frenchman and I because we were such good friends. I have no idea how he worded it, but it made perfect sense at the time.

The young Frenchman (he might have even been younger than me) chose the shorter lady, so the other one led me off into the dark streets of a largely sleeping island town. There were sparse street lights, each with its ball of misty air around it, and the streets were far too narrow for cars. A small trickle of water ran down the gutter on both sides, and everything was damp with an old, musty smell. The air was misty, and to an Illinois boy the whole thing seemed surreal.

There appeared to be separate buildings with common walls, so there was no break in the walls along the street. We didn't talk at all, I just followed, listening to our footsteps on the bricks in the dark. We finally reached a door right on the street, and entered a small room, with only a bed, a table, a lantern, and a basin.

She took off her clothes and laid down on the bed. I remember feeling like I was trying to keep up with an unknown script. Not knowing what else to do, I took off my clothes and sat next to her. I remember being very surprised at how firm her breasts were, and years later, realized that she was probably horribly young for that occupation.

Afterward, with no embarrassment at all, she squatted over a small basin and urinated, and then dumped the basin into the gutter on the street. I guessed that was a kind of primitive birth control, and understood that what I had assumed were gutters were open sewers. I followed her back to the bar in silence.

She didn't come in, and walked off into the darkness without a word. Going into the bar was like rejoining the real world. The young Frenchman was there with Ted, going on and on about the fact that the lady he went with had a red light. Why that impressed him so much I don't know. Perhaps his English wasn't good enough to convey the reason, or perhaps I lost his words in between drinks.

The world was a much safer place then. There was no Aids, Herpes was virtually unknown, and the south Florida drug industry was still in its infancy. While I was a little concerned on that dim walk about robbery, I had no concerns of being robbed and killed. Although in retrospect, the chances of either happening to Ted's guest would be minimal.

Since then, I have reflected on perspective. I doubt very much that she even remembers that night. But for me, it was a journey into an unknown world, a, damp, dark, mysterious and forbidden zone. And I have thought, since then, that we never know how much damage we do on this earth, we can only hope it is not too much.

Asking the right question

Asking the right question has become a real soapbox of mine. The attitude with which we approach a question or a problem can predestine failure or maximize the chance for success. I guess part of the right attitude is a willingness to challenge assumptions, assumptions we may not even know that we are making.

At a very early age I was given a graphic example of the need to "ask the right question". One of my earliest memories is trying to color in five of twelve ducks on a page when it was success for me to get the crayon to the page at all. At the end of third grade the Cerebral Palsy I have had since an illness shortly after birth was preventing me from writing legibly. The neighborhood grade school reluctantly informed my folks that since I couldn't write, I could not go on to fourth grade.

The question the school had asked was a simple one: can he go on to fourth grade? The answer was also simple: if he cannot write legibly, then he cannot go on to fourth grade (it has always intrigued me that this criterion would seemingly keep a large proportion of medical doctors stuck in third grade).

This was well before the advent of special education, and I would have simply stayed home. My folks, along with the local United Cerebral Palsy affiliate, asked a different question: how can he go on to fourth grade? The school was approached with another question: if he can learn to type, can he bring a typewriter to school and go on to fourth grade? And so it was that a single grade school principal said yes to full inclusion by the implementation of assistive technology decades before those terms existed.

Not too many years later the local YMCA tried to teach me to swim. In fairness to the YMCA, allegedly the crawl is the easiest stroke for most folks to learn after the dog paddle (assuming the dog paddle can be called a stroke—a swimming stroke, not either of the other kinds). I think I was around 9 years old.

They tried for at least two separate classes, maybe three. Apparently it was written in marble (an apt reference for my early attempts at swimming), beginning swimmers learned the crawl. My crawl stroke has not changed in 40 odd years.

If I concentrate on arms, shoulders, and breathing, my flutter kick fades to a few jerks. At that point, my legs sink and I am trying to pull myself through the water with my legs hanging almost straight down, not a very efficient position (years later, when I took hydrodynamics, I learned the scientific words to pin on that common sense idea). If I concentrate on my flutter kick, my arms kind of fade, my head doesn't clear the water, and I can "swim" only as long as I can hold my breath.

The crawl just takes too many muscles at once. In addition, for most all of my life, I have been negatively buoyant (I sink in water). For those of you who wish you were thin, there is a downside to everything!

Anyway, the appointed day of the test came, and they lined us up at the deep end. The balcony was filled with parents. I don't know about the other kids, but I shivered and felt naked and afraid. One by one, kids jumped in. Some, most I think, swam the length and passed the course. Some jumped in and could only swim part way before grabbing the side. In the first case, the parents applauded with gusto. In the second, the parents applauded politely.

Then, it was my turn. I knew I couldn't swim. The instructors knew I couldn't swim. Maybe the instructors had the same fantasy hope that I did. Somehow, with a balcony full of parents, on the final day, I would have an epiphany and become a "swimmer." Regardless, I was too young to do other than what I was told to do.

I jumped in. I probably, in retrospect, panicked. We had never done anything in the deep end. I had never been taught the dead man's float nor any survival skills. I had only been taught the crawl, which I couldn't do.

I remember the seemingly thousands of bubbles which followed me into the water. I remember watching them leave me as they went up and I went down. I remember the pole piercing the water, dragging its own compliment of bubbles down. I remember grabbing the pole, literally for dear life, and being hauled out, broken and disgraced. I remember slipping and sliding, as the balcony sat in silence, while I ran for the showers. My mom has told me that that was the only time she ever saw me cry in public.

Since then I have done underwater marine cathodic inspections in Brazil, and a study of marine coral cave fauna in Bermuda. In Carleton College, I swam a mile three times a week for fun and exercise--never a crawl, of course...but the YMCA couldn't teach me to swim. Why? Because they asked the wrong question. They never asked "how can we teach this kid to swim?" They only asked "can we teach this kid to swim?"

More on asking the right question later...

Bumble bees

I admit it: I don't like bumble bees! I am sure they perform a function on this earth, but I prefer that they perform their function far away from me. In fact, I have a longstanding feud with bumbles, kind of an inter-specific vendetta.

When I lived on Granddad's farm, once in a while I would hunt bumble bees. He had an old breach loading 22 rifle, used so much it was practically a smooth bore, and I would load a 22 shell filled with tiny shot. It was truly a single shot, and reloading required a knife, to get the casing out far enough you could grab it with a pair of pliers, also required.

Bumbles are perhaps the most dangerous small game on earth. Trying to find and finish a wounded bumble in a bean field is dangerous, nerve wracking work. But hey, if you're going to bumble hunt, you have to have the right stuff!

Perhaps my feud started one afternoon when I was mowing the barnyard. The mower was a self propelled power mower, and I enjoyed the 3 hour task. That was long enough ago that the mower didn't have a dead man's kill bar to tie wrap up to the handle, so I just meandered along behind the mower, one hand lightly on the handle, enjoying the sun and the wind, the noise of the mower sheltering my thoughts and enclosing me in my "mower space."

On that fateful afternoon, however, toward the middle of the barnyard, suddenly I was surrounded by bumbles. I froze. I wish that I could claim it was a strategy, but it was just surprise and fear. The mower trundled on across the yard, completely oblivious to the fury around us. The bumbles, about twelve in all, followed the mower, and I watched then zipping around it and occasionally darting in to sting.

I ducked down (I have no idea why, it just seemed right to duck) and ran back to the gravel driveway. I think I waited about five minutes before I went and retrieved the mower from the ditch it had ended up in. Then, very cautiously, I began watching the area where it had started.

Well, it turned out the bumbles had commandeered a chipmunk tunnel. I presume it had been empty, but I wouldn't put it past bumbles to have evicted a family of sweet, lovable, chipmunks!

Well, chipmunks anyway (chipmunks are considered varmints, and I shot them too if they began tearing up the ground under the house or the garage).

Anyway, we had a nest of bumbles in the barnyard, and I knew where it was, so I went and told Granddad. He looked very thoughtful and simply said "Ok." Granddad never said much until years later, when his hearing was gone. Then, after a while at a family dinner, he would start talking just to participate, and go on and on and on....

But again, I digress. I was anxious to learn what he was going to do. The barnyard was broken, it had a nest of bumbles in it, and I knew Granddad would fix it. That's what Granddad did when something was broken, he fixed it. I was thinking a glorious attack with gasoline, fire bombing them, or maybe backing up a cement truck and cementing the suckers over, forever entombing them in their stolen chipmunk property.

So I was very surprised when he came out of the garage uncoiling an extension cord. What in the world was he up to? He crossed the nearly 50 feet to the bumble entrance, and then walked off into the house.

After a few minutes, he came out carrying Grandma's canister vacuum cleaner! He plugged it in, carefully put the end of the hose right next to the bumble hole opening, and then turned it on. Then he watched. A bumble on the way out, no doubt with mayhem on its mind, surfaced and fssst, he was vacuumed. A bumble returning, no doubt from doing mayhem, tried to enter and fssst, he was vacuumed too! Satisfied, Granddad walked back to the garage, leaving the vacuum on, and whatever he had been doing when I interrupted him with the news that the barnyard was broken.

I went back to mowing that part of the barnyard that wasn't broken. It wasn't quite the same, though. My "mower space" had been rudely violated, and the daydreams and wandering thoughts wouldn't quite push aside the constant awareness of a bumble war in process.

After a couple hours, Granddad went to the house and came out with a spray can of insect killer. By then, there were no bumbles to be seen, either coming or going, but the canister vacuum cleaner had a second buzzing louder than the motor. With the vacuum still running, Granddad simply sprayed the aerosol into the hose. In about 3 minutes, the bumble buzzing stopped. And the barnyard had been fixed!

Grandma wasn't too happy about it, but hey, life's all about trade offs, right?

Indiana Oopsie

We all pick up things as we trudge, walk, or skip through life. Little chunks of experience and stuff. Experience can clutter the mind as stuff can clutter the parlor. Stuff we can throw away. Experience, hopefully, we can learn from. Sometimes, of course, we get both experience and stuff from the same event.

It was the very early 70's in a small college in Indiana. I was a freshman, living in a college dorm. My roommate, John, was a big, gangly man who played twelve string Rickenbacher guitar. He loved to play rhythm. He brought with him two five foot Fender speakers and an amplifier to power them, all band quality equipment. We spent many enjoyable hours jamming, me on harmonica and John on guitar. Well, enjoyable for us, anyway.

Those of us who lived in the dorm were misfits, most of the students lived in fraternities or sororities. We were either those who chose not to pledge to a fraternity or those who were never asked to join. A motley crew, but an interesting one.

The early 70's, you may remember if you are as old as I am, were interesting and dynamic years. The Vietnam war was in full swing, as was the movement against it. The draft, also, was in full swing. While I believed that the war was wrong (mistake might be a better word), I did not believe it qualified for civil disobedience. In this way, I managed to offend almost everyone who had strong opinions about the war (I learned in high school that if both sides are mad at you, you're probably doing something right—but that is another story).

I also believed that college deferments were wrong, simply a way for the wealthy to side step ending up a private on the front line, so I didn't apply for one. I received a very high number in the lottery (each year, a lottery was held to determine an order of draft, by birthday—my number was well above 300) though, so it didn't matter. It was a time when R.O.T.C. buildings were being burned and older folks were deeply offended by Jimmy Hendrix's rendition of the Star Spangled Banner. Geez, I am now older than many of those "older folks!"

Anyway, I got along well with my roommate. He didn't mind that every night I hung his tennis shoes out the window, even in

27

winter. I did this not out of meanness, but out of self-defense. The word "odiferous" does not begin to describe John's tennis shoes.

The college was on a modified semester system, with a one month interim period between first and second semesters for independent study and in-depth projects. The first semester passed without particular incident, except for recurring ill health for me. I went home at Christmas, and Doc Hart decided that I had never really recovered from the mononucleosis of senior year in high school, so I stayed home for the one month interim period and worked on something or other independently.

So it was that I returned to the small college in the small town in Indiana for the second semester, having missed a month of school. I had only been back a few days when John came into our room, followed by an older man in a huge green army coat. John told him that "I was cool" and the man began counting out money. John produced a cylinder wrapped in aluminum foil. It was an obvious drug deal, and I was annoyed only because I felt "our room" was being used without my consent.

The man turned to leave, but when he got to the door, he turned around with a huge pistol aimed at us. At that point in my life, I had never seen a hand gun, except in passing in the holsters of uniformed police officers. My first thought was that it was a robbery, and he would simply shoot us, and walk away with the money and the drugs.

I was so relieved when he arrested us! I suppose I put my hands up, but I don't remember. I only remember what it felt like looking at a gun aimed my way. He had us put on our coats, and told us that he wouldn't embarrass us with handcuffs if we would "come quietly." Later, I figured out that he wanted to protect his anonymity, not avoid embarrassment for us.

Anyway, I put on my almost full length black fake fur coat, and my little black Russian style cap, and off we went to jail. It was, I believe, late afternoon.

I don't remember being finger printed and all that, but I am sure that I was. I do remember, as they went down a checklist, that they asked about medical conditions and I listed Cerebral Palsy. Once I said no medication was needed, I am sure they forgot it. John and I ended up in an empty cell block, about 10 4 person cells, all open, with a long common area inside the outer bars. Everyone else in jail was in the other cell block. I expect they were all locals, and have no idea who the jailors thought they were protecting, but I was very glad John and I were segregated.

After a bit we were brought down together to the sheriff's office to make our phone call. I will never understand why, but a number of deputies and their wives appeared to have collected to watch this event. John went first, and his was a tearful, broken, and disjointed call home. The more distraught he became, the more his audience appeared to enjoy it. I began to be truly concerned about John and very annoyed with his audience.

Then it was my turn. How do you tell your parents that you've just been arrested for four drug related felonies? Since each one carried a maximum sentence of 20 years, we were looking at an 80 year maximum!

My mom answered the phone, and I think I started out with something bland like "Mom, I've got some bad news." Realizing there just isn't an easy way into the fact that you now have a long rap sheet, I just told her straight up of the arrest. Bless her heart, her only question was "Did you do it?"

At this point I turned a little to look the sheriff straight in the eye as I answered her. "No, I did not, and you send the lawyers and we'll pay the rest of my way through school at the expense of these jerks." I was young, and angry, and worried about John, but for all of that, that was a singularly stupid thing to do. I think right then they decided I must be from a crime family or mafia or something.

Then it was back to the cell block. I should add that there was never any abuse of any kind. Except for wanting to put us away for most of our lives, our jailers were remarkably civil.

I was quite concerned about John, who was horribly despondent. I made light of whatever I could. There were no sheets nor pillows nor blankets in any of the cells, but lots of thin mattresses, so we used a mattress for a mattress, a mattress for a pillow, and a mattress for a blanket. During the mattress collection project, we found a small round plastic thing, I forget what, maybe the top from a peanut butter jar.

So I created a modified shuffle board game we could play in the common area inside our cell block, sliding this thing across the concrete floor, maybe thirty feet, I would guess. We played that until someone on the other side (we couldn't see them) yelled for us to stop.

It was time to go to bed. I remember quipping to John that we finally had singles! In the dorm, no one but dorm assistants had singles. We had chosen adjacent cells in the center of our cell block, and a single light bulb hung from a wire just out of my reach.

I knew John, quite a bit taller than me, could unscrew the bulb easily. So I asked him if he would do it. Remember, we were in jail charged with four felonies and looking at potentially 80 years in prison. When I asked him to unscrew that light bulb, he looked at me and said, in total sincerity, "I don't want to get into trouble?"

It was too much. I laughed so loudly that we heard again from someone in the other cell block. Such was my first (and last) night in an Indiana jail.

I am a very firm believer in both perspective and confidence. With perspective you can find humor in the worst situations, and with confidence you can enjoy the humor you find. The two together form a tremendous defense of sanity.

Indiana in process

My glimpse into the legal system of the time was a very interesting one. For me, one lesson learned is that it is no better nor worse than any system administered by people.

The next day I had a hearing in the afternoon. In Indiana at that time, there was no arraignment process. The individual prosecuting attorney made the call whether or not to proceed to trial. I did not know it at the time, but this was going to become very important later on. The judge was quite elderly, with thick glasses and of course, a black robe. My dad was there with my uncle, and I had representation from a local lawyer. I later learned my mom had stayed in Peoria to be ready to shuffle money around for bail.

And then I was out of jail. The legal process began grinding along. My lawyer deposed (got testimony under oath) from the sheriff and I assume the arresting officer. I learned later they continued questioning John, and tried very hard to get him to say that I was involved.

John and I were frequent headliners in the college newspaper. Since the college newspaper went to parents and alumni as well, the administration took a hard line stance, and promised all a thorough review of the matter when the courts were done. This annoyed me to no end, because the college highlighted its function as en loco parentis in its catalogue and promotional material, yet they were of zero help to John, to me, or to either family, choosing instead to stand with arms folded and wait to pass judgment. Somehow, I kept going to class.

I was home, Easter recess I think, when the offers began coming. The first was to plead guilty to a misdemeanor and get no time in prison, only probation. I should mention here that the town, which would produce the jury if we did go to trial, did not like the college. It was a time when America was deeply divided, largely by age. The jurors would be old (say--older than 30) and I was young. To the first offer we said no.

Our lawyer had explained that the sworn testimony of the sheriff described a picture perfect false arrest. In theory, if we sued, we could walk in, hand the judge the sworn testimony of the sheriff, and win. It is who we would sue that made it interesting. At that time, in Indiana, because the prosecutor made the call to proceed, it would be the prosecutor that we would sue, not the state. So we began a high stakes negotiation process.

The next offer was that I would come down, with my hair cut, and the charges would be dismissed in open court, and we would sign an agreement not to sue for false arrest. Someone, Dad or Mom, had the sense to ask why this wouldn't be handled by paperwork only, and did they intend to say in court, on the record, that I was guilty but they couldn't prove it. Our lawyer seemed ashamed of the court, but admitted that that was almost certainly the plan. For the second time, we said no.

The last offer we accepted. Nothing would be said in open court, we would visit with the judge in his chambers, and we would agree not to sue. We wanted to talk privately to the judge, probably a great deal more than he wanted to talk to us.

At the hearing almost nothing was said, just formalities. Charges were dropped and things were signed. Then my mom, dad and I entered the judges chambers.

The judge opened up with the comment that I was headed for trouble, and that at the initial hearing, after I had been in jail nearly 24 hours, he could tell by my eyes that I was under the influence of narcotics. My mom handed the judge a letter written by Doctor Hart, who had been my doctor for 19 years, and who had recommended that I stay home during the interim term to regain my health (yes, I admit it, on more than one occasion, I drove myself to see my pediatrician, but that's another story).

In sum and substance, the letter said that even Doctor Hart, my doctor since infancy, could not distinguish the symptoms of drugs or alcohol with certainty without blood tests, because my kind of Cerebral Palsy can so closely mimic either. The judge read, and I suspect reread, for a rather long time. At this point in my life, I give the judge real credit. He did something which many, many people cannot do.

In the presence of new information, he changed his mind. He recommended that I keep a copy of that letter in my wallet, and he and my mom had a fairly lengthy, friendly discussion about the difficulty of fair treatment by the criminal system, from police to judges, of individuals with disabilities. All in all, it was pleasantly anti-climactic.

At the time, of course, I saw good guys and bad guys. Now I remember just people, with the normal human spectrum of intelligence and ethics. The sheriff did not lie; the judge did change his mind. All in all, I feel very lucky, even though I had done nothing wrong, at least not what I had been charged with.

So ok, what stuff did I get? I got an arrest record of four felonies. What did I learn? The power of truth and family and the freaky nature of timing. As it happened, I did not have time to be guilty. My family mobilized and by the time it was all done, I am certain the authorities and the administration were breathing sighs of relief more than us. But in truth, if I had witnessed a sale before the last sale, I would not have turned John in. I might have been annoyed, but I would not have turned him in. And in that event, I would have been guilty.

It also did not escape my notice that the name of the sheriff was 'Bob". I know that, because his name was stitched onto an oval patch sewn on his shirt.

On Bob

A few years ago I wrote the following piece and sent it off to COMPUTERWORLD, more or less the premiere computer industry weekly. They said that they liked it but couldn't use it. Unfortunately, the editors there completely missed the point of the treatise. They thought it was a commentary on computer obsolescence, when in fact it is a sojourn into the world of Bobs.

I don't know what it is about that name, Bob, that makes it beg to be stitched onto an oval patch on a pair of coveralls, but it does. It practically demands it. Perhaps because it is the same name frontward and backward (a very useful quality for words on license plates, by the way). It's a nice name, and lest I be accused of prejudice, I even have a friend named Bob--sort of a friend, anyway.

- -

My "new" car was three years old, and running a little rough. It was my pride and joy, so I immediately went back to the dealer. The initial news was great, "It's only a spark plug." said Bob, in the green coveralls.

"Great!" I said. "How long to fix it?"

Bob looked thoughtful, and checked his computer. He began to look concerned, and I had the first inklings of fear. "They've improved the plug design." he said.

"What does that mean?" I asked, thinking I now probably had to buy a set.

"Well, they burn hotter for cleaner combustion. They also last longer."

"What's it mean, Bob?"

"Well, the good news is your car will run better than it did when it was new, and be better for the environment."

"It ran fine last week, Bob. And...?"

Bob frowned now, studying the screen intently. "Well, the bad news is that because they burn hotter we'll have to coat the piston heads with a heat resistant material. But your crankshafts aren't strong enough for the added energy, so we'll have to swap those out. Let me check... "

"I was afraid of that. The new crankshafts will require a new drive shaft, but the new drive shafts aren't compatible with your transmission, sorry."

"Hold on a second! It's only a spark plug!"

"I know," said Bob, looking like he truly felt my pain. "But if we put in a new transmission, the front axle, tie rods, wheels, brakes, and u-joints will also have to be replaced."

Fortunately, at that point I woke up in a cold sweat. Thank heavens it was only a dream! As I showered and dressed for work I thanked Congress for the ten year parts available law for automobiles.

My first call was a simple one. My client described a problem with his three year old network and I said "No sweat. It's just a Network Interface Card (NIC). I'll be right over."

The rest of the day was a good one. My client was gracious about the fact that we couldn't buy a NIC compatible with his old system, so we ended up upgrading the network software, which required a complete upgrade of his other hardware. By the end of the day, his system was up and much better than before, as well as being Y2K ready.

With a sigh of heartfelt relief, my client said "Thanks, Bob."

Sometimes, things are written just for fun!

Judi and a poem for Lisa

Judi was the first great love of my life. It was an all consuming, almost unhealthy love. Time away from her was simply time waiting to be near her. I met her at Ted's wedding, when I was living on Tropic in Hypoluxo and she was living in Sunrise, just west of Ft. Lauderdale. And I met her when the world was young.

Judi told me she would teach me to play backgammon while we ate cake at Ted's wedding. After a long time, I screwed up my courage and called her to ask her to dinner. It was easy and wonderful. In no time at all, I was in love.

Her problems were more important than my problems. She was raising two daughters alone, and facing down the world. She had a wild history, she had partied with the Miami Dolphins in their heydays and done things I had only dreamed about. It seemed she knew the "real" world, in ways I could only imagine.

I got to know her daughters, Leslie and Lisa. Leslie, dark and beautiful and mischievous, was the younger. Lisa had long flowing beautiful blond hair, and a quick wit.

I remember getting a call from Judi in the wee hours of the morning, and going with her to a swamp at dawn, looking for them at a house owned by a rich family and used by their sons. I moved her away from the door, and kicked it in. The girls were there, and when property damage came up, so did statutory rape, and we simply took the girls and left.

Ultimately, I took her home to meet the family in Peoria, Illinois, at Christmas. By then I was running a boat refurbishing business and working on an engineering degree at Florida Atlantic University. She was like a child playing in the Illinois snow. I had dreams of a forever together.

When we returned to Florida, everything changed overnight, literally. There was no "we" and no explanation. It was like "we" had never happened. I was devastated. I did so badly that FAU suspended me for a semester.

For nearly a semester, I was a basket case. I would hobble around campus (I had a plantar wart on my right heel) and talk to anyone who would listen about Judi. I know now I must have been terribly boring, and thank those who bothered to listen.

I began seeing my future wife and pulling myself back together. I went in to see my Statics and Dynamics professor a week before the term was to end. It was, I think, the first time he had seen me! He told me that I mathematically couldn't pass the course, but I took the comprehensive final anyway. It really annoyed him when I scored one of the highest scores, but true to his word, he failed me anyway.

It was the term before graduation during finals when Judi called me from Missouri. The girls had been visiting their Dad. There had been a terrible accident. Two boys and two girls (Leslie and Lisa) out in a jeep ran a stop sign in front of a cement truck. Leslie went 50 feet through the air, landed in a bush, and walked away virtually unscathed. The jeep rolled over on Lisa, and nearly severed her leg.

When the life flight arrived at the hospital, Lisa had no blood pressure at all. The doctors did what they could. When there was no circulation to her toes, they cut them off. When her foot died, they cut it off. Across nearly a week, they just cut more and more of her off.

Judi called and asked me to come. I had spent more than a year rebuilding my life. I said no. That decision still bothers me. Even the nurses cried when they washed and combed her beautiful hair, the day before she died. When they cut off her thigh, I think Lisa just gave up.

I wanted to go there, and will her to live. But I didn't. I wanted to go there and promise to teach her to SCUBA dive with one leg, but I didn't. I wanted to go there and make her see that beauty isn't about two legs, and life doesn't have to be all about walking, but I didn't.

I didn't.

Sometimes there are no pearls of wisdom, and no lessons learned, except, perhaps, that we all make mistakes.

After this was written, I sent it to Judi. Yep, we still talk. But that's another story. This was her response.

Dear John,
Thanks for sending the chapter on Lisa and myself. It is amazing how differently people remember events in their lives. One thing for sure, I

knew I loved you but I also knew I would not be good for you. I knew I would hurt you and I never wanted to do that. I will write later about how I remember that chapter and the errors in Lisa's death but that was very beautiful John. I never knew you loved me that much. I loved you equally but wasn't ready for such a wonderful man. I just knew I would hurt you. You did the right thing. As for not coming when Lisa died you should not feel bad. There is really nothing you could have done. She wanted the truth from you and the truth was that she was dying. Who would want that burden. I know she asked for you because you wouldn't lie.
Love, Judi

I had totally forgotten that Lisa asked for me to go there, and Judi simply relayed the request. Remembering, once upon a time, I was that honest and that strong. It feels sometimes like I am struggling to recover that me, after years of wear and tear. But such is life, I guess.

The North Atlantic Enraged

I have always loved nature in all her forms, from the simply beautiful to the truly spectacular. The North Atlantic Ocean is a place of all shades of nature, and I treasure my memories of time spent there.

It was a grey day, with the winds picking up to forty knots or so. The hurricane was off the east coast of the U.S. and headed our way. Our unlimited marine license captain was sequestered in radio room trying to convince the rig manager to evacuate the rig.

One of the regulatory changes following the Ocean Ranger disaster was that we had to have a Captain on board with an Unlimited License, meaning he was licensed to captain an ocean liner across the seas. Ours was an American, who knew nothing about oil rigs. I did wonder what dark disaster in his past made him willing to "captain" a vessel that virtually never went anywhere.

The Barge Engineer was in Barge Control coordinating with the driller and rig superintendent as they prepared to "hang off" the drill pipe so the rig could disconnect from the BOP stack. The sea was already running 20 to 30 feet high, and the barometer was doing a nose dive. The warehouseman and a few other administrative personnel had already gone to the beach.

I spoke with the crane operator, and he agreed to begin tying things down, using his crew of roustabouts. He also agreed to run hand lines along major pathways on deck for hands to hang onto if necessary. A couple of hours later he came to see me.

They were stopped in their work because they had used every bit of rope and chain they had available, and the warehouse was locked. The warehouseman was already on the beach, so they couldn't get more rope or chain. Together, we walked out on the port deck.

The warehouse was above the welding shop. Now I admit, it's a warehouseman's job to be stingy, at least enough to stop the wanton waste of material. But some warehousemen took to that task with more glee than others. Suffice it say that the crane op, the roustabouts, and I all took satisfaction when I had us pick up a torch on the way up the steps to the warehouse hatch, and just cut off the large padlock.

Supplied, the crew went back to work stringing hand lines and tying things down. Somewhere in this time the drill crew hung off the drill pipe in the BOP, shut in the well, and disconnected the riser from the BOP. The wind and seas were slowly rising, and a decision was made to cut crew down to a bare minimum skeleton crew.

The vast majority of the approximately eighty hands were lowered in a personnel basket to a waiting supply boat. I think about 10 of us remained on board. The weather had gotten to the point where if we waited longer, it would not be safe to offload personnel to a boat. Anyway, we offloaded most of the crew and they set off on the nearly 20 hour boat trip to St. Johns.

There were two reasons we wanted a crew on board, both stemming from a feeling that the rig was "ours" and should not be left defenseless. In bad weather there are steps operators can take to help the vessel against the storm, and there was also concern that if the rig were abandoned, Russian sailors could board and claim rights of salvage.

I put on my deck gear and went to walk a round on deck, taking a roustabout with me. My deck gear included an elastic strap for my glasses and a hard hat, also with an elastic chin strap. I was proud of that hard hat, white plastic with a couple years worth of oilfield stickers on it.

The wind was on the port bow, so we went out the upper aft exit of the quarters, onto the walkway (sans toe rails) that ringed the quarters, and headed to port. It was almost calm aft of the quarters, and I think we both were almost strolling when we reached the corner. I rounded the corner and almost blew over, lost my hard hat and just barely caught my glasses as the wind ripped them right off my face!

There is nothing that I have ever seen to compare with the sheer energy of the North Atlantic in a major storm. We were nervously laughing as we returned to the quarters for another hard hat, and then resumed our deck walk far more cautiously. By now the ocean was streaking, long white lines running across the waves. Waves never totally break at sea. Waves crest and break only when a shallowing bottom pushes the wave higher until it crests and falls over itself.

The average seas now were forty to fifty feet high. Since the main deck was fifty feet above sea level, it was spectacular but didn't feel dangerous. And, of course, as a wave passed the rig, the rig climbed, or floated up, the wave. The rig was rated for 110 foot seas.

We were crossing the open area on the port deck heading for the welding shop when the roustabout grabbed my arm. Talking was impossible because of the wind, but he shouted "Look!" and pointed to port. The port side of the rig was in a wave trough, and when I looked to port the oncoming wave top was way higher than main deck. The roustabout bolted for the quarters.

I was about ten feet away from the port guard rail, and fifty feet away from the quarters hatch. For a few seconds I debated what to do. The guard rail was made from retired drill pipe, a double row of 9" diameter steel pipe, and it was not going anywhere, wave or no wave. If we did get blue water over the main deck, and I was not inside the quarters, I could possibly get washed over the side. So I ran to the guard rail, wrapping legs and arms around it.

Wrapped around the guard rail, the wind screaming and lesser waves running down the huge swell as it came at us, I felt the awesome power and fury of nature. I could feel the rig begin to climb as the leading edge of the swell passed under me. My glasses were covered with sea spray but it didn't matter, all of the players in this drama were huge, fine details of sight were not needed. I screamed into the wind, encouraging the rig to climb. There was no fear, just excitement and pride in my rig as she shuddered and climbed. The top of the swell passed about ten feet below main deck, and the whole rig shook as the swell hammered the 30 foot diameter corner columns, and the garage size anchor windlasses vanished in foam.

The entire time was probably less than a minute. For me, it was as close as I ever want to get to an angry North Atlantic, and closer than I want to get ever again, but I still relish that minute and it's memory. The power and energy was simply awesome. My rig, so huge and powerful and stable, was being shifted about like a chunk of wood, heaving and listing and yawing.

The next swell was well away and smaller, and I quickly returned to quarters, shutting down deck walkabouts for the duration. Anything not already secured would simply have to fend for itself. It just wasn't worth the risk.

In the end, they didn't let us stay, and we had to totally abandon the rig, going to St. Johns by chopper. Those of us who had stayed on board made out like the proverbial bandits. We beat the boat in by many hours, and later learned that most of our people on board were horribly seasick, and one man broke his leg and two men broke arms during that very rough trip to town (floating oil rigs are designed to be stable for drilling, so none of us had real sea legs).

I will never forget that minute on the guard rail, praying and wishing and trying by sheer will to force the rig to climb that wave in time. Never, before or since, have I felt so tiny and so energized at once.

Sometimes today, when I am in a meeting where advocates are demanding "complete safety" for individuals with disabilities, I remember that minute, and reflect that no one should deny another the opportunity for their own personal adventures, whether it's clinging to a guard rail, or walking by themselves to a corner store to buy something. Life is not safe, and sometimes the best experiences include risk.

The Ocean Ranger and aftermath

Occasionally, events dictate turns in our lives, probably more often than we like to believe. In early 1982, I had been working for Sedco Inc., based in Dallas Texas, for a little over a year as an Engineer Trainee. I was commuting, and would fly from Peoria, Illinois to St. John's, Newfoundland, work four weeks on the Sedco 706, an offshore drilling rig, and then fly back to Peoria for 4 weeks off. It's actually quite a nice way to work, with six months off a year.

In Peoria, I would get my truck, a Dodge mini ram pickup, out of storage, get my dog out of the kennel, and drive non-stop to Connecticut to stay with my girlfriend. I was in Connecticut on February 15th, 1982. I think it was early that afternoon when I got a call from Bob P, the assistant Rig Manager. His message was simple: get on a plane and get back to St. John immediately. The Ocean Ranger had rolled over and sunk, losing all hands. 84 men had died.

The Ocean Ranger was one of three rigs working at that time for a consortium of oil companies on the Grand Banks. The Sedco 706 and the Xapata Ugland were the other two. The two remaining rigs had been ordered to Marystown Shipyard, which is why I got called. I had worked on a BOP (Blow Out Preventer) refit in the shipyard, and knew the yard and the personnel.

The truck and the dog stayed with my girlfriend, who also became my fiancée that day. She agreed to marry me as soon as I got back, whenever that would be. Clearing Canadian immigration was actually pleasant. The man wished me good luck instead of glaring suspiciously at my papers. The loss of the Ranger was huge news, and he knew why I was en route.

By the time I got to St. John's, both rigs were underway to Marystown. It was, I think, an understandable knee jerk reaction to a disaster which wasn't totally understood. The decision was, I think, to shut down, remove risk, until what had happened was better understood.

That night, at the Chalet Inn, it sunk in to me that I would never know which faces had died. All three rigs had shared services. We shared chopper flights to the rigs. We were all quartered during crew changes at the Chalet Inn, a motel on the outskirts of town. We would eat, drink, play video games and such the night before crew change. I knew, at best, the first names of guys from the Ranger. The ones who had been off at the time had no reason to come back, their rig was gone. The ones who had been on, of course, were dead.

The next day Jean, the office administrator, gave me the keys to a rental car. Even she was subdued. She was a small, feisty gal, who loved picking on engineers.

I had a small window of weather to get to Marystown. West on the Trans-Canada highway, and then left down the Marystown Peninsula highway. I found out later that people who left hours after me arrived days later. It was cloudy and cold, but without rain or snow when I left.

En route, I learned about front wheel drive. I had never driven a front wheel drive car before. Going up a small hill, and around a gentle curve to the left, I hit black ice. I did what I always did on ice, taking my foot off the gas but not braking.

That was a bad idea. The car fishtailed to the right, and I corrected. It fishtailed left, and I corrected. While I slid gently into the oncoming traffic lane, down the small incline some highway engineer had added for the curve, the back end swung right again, this time all the way around and I went back end first off the road and into a snow bank.

The car stalled, and I sat there for a moment in complete silence. I think my first reaction was that MY rig was coming in I needed to be there to meet it. I got out and walked around the car, picking up the plastic mud guard thingy that had been under the engine compartment and putting it in the back seat.

It was quite a while later I figured out what had happened. On ice, in a rear wheel drive car, taking your foot off the accelerator adds just a touch of differential drag on the rear tires, and you track a little better. In a front wheel drive, doing that adds a little braking power on the front wheels, which is not a good thing to do on ice.

The car started and drove out. I didn't even think about how lucky I was, I was just concerned about getting to Marystown. I did learn, on the peninsula road, what the weird plow contraptions were. Plows had a fork lift type thing on the front. The peninsula road was like driving in a narrow canyon, with snow walls ten feet high on both sides. The plows could, when needed, lift the blade, cantilever it sideways, and plow the top of the plowed snow further off the road.

Both rigs were at anchor when I got to Marystown. Marystown is a nearly perfect harbor, with a very narrow entrance between very high rock walls, sheltered on all sides with a broad expanse inside. It was strange to see two huge ocean dwellers so close to land and so close to each other. The rigs sat at anchor, with small ice chunks (5 to 10 feet) floating around the harbor.

I checked in the hotel (the Marystown Hotel, of course) and set my two hand radios up in the charger. I contacted the rig, using marine channel 6, which we always used. The radio op explained that marine channel 6 is not for use on the shore, so he gave me the call sign "Seagull" hoping that sounded like a boat. Yet today, I can hear the rhythm of calling the rig, "706, 706, Seagull…" In the weeks to come I would say that dozens of times a day.

During the next 6 weeks we did a Type 4 (the most thorough) inspection, installed new lifeboats, and made some other minor changes while the regulators, the oil companies, and the operators (us) talked about ways to ensure that a catastrophe like the Ranger never happened again. The press also descended on Marystown. And that taught me the power of a "thank you."

After the BOP project, I sent a telex (yes, we still used telexes) to the Operational Manager of the shipyard expressly to thank and express our appreciation for the security force. They had gone way out of their way to be helpful and friendly as we worked oilfield hours and came and went all hours of the day and night. Of course, I copied the security office too, even though I never expected to return.

I was the only Sedco man on the beach, and had explicit instructions to say nothing to the press. When the press were touring the yard, on more than one occasion, the security force kept me appraised by radio of where they were, so I could be elsewhere. That simple thank you gave me a team of support I never had dreamed I would need or use.

Anyway, as the work progressed slowly more information about what had happened came to light. Think of an oil rig as a huge table standing on two submarines. The 706 had corner columns which were 130 feet high and 30 feet in diameter. The quarters, two stories high, sat forward, the pipe deck and mud house aft, with the derrick and drill deck in the middle above the "moon pool", a large opening in the deck where the riser went to the BOP on the sea floor.

On the Ocean Ranger, Barge Control was below the main deck. Barge Control is the center for all operations that have to do with the fact that the rig is also a vessel. Keeping trim, proper ballasting, marine radio and radar all are centered in Barge Control. Every Barge Control has a ballast control panel.

The control panel controls the ballast pumps and the ballast tank valves remotely. The ballast tanks are located inside the hulls, so if you're taking cargo on the starboard side, an operator can pump water out of a ballast tank on the starboard side, and keep the rig in balance. There is a lot more to it, but that is the essence. The main job of Barge Control is to keep a floating rig floating.

A few days before the Ranger sank a huge wave had broken a port hole in Barge Control, and had put sea water in the ballast control panel. Apparently the crew on board had thought they had it fixed, but they were wrong. On the night the Ranger sank, it was stormy, but it was not the storm that sank the Ranger. Ballast valves began opening and closing on their own, and she began to trim down at the bow (she tipped forward).

There are many questions that will never be answered. The Ranger did not sink in a hurry. She slowly tipped further and further forward. She got at least one lifeboat away, but many in the boat were not even fully dressed. A supply boat spotted the lifeboat, and went as close as she dared in the heavy seas.

The men inside the lifeboat didn't follow the training they should have had, and did not stay in their seats, seat belts on. At that time, and probably still today, the biggest threat to an oil rig is a blow out and fire, and that was the threat behind life boat design. Rig lifeboats are totally enclosed, motorized, with a sprinkler system so that even if the boat is navigating through floating burning oil, it has a chance.

On that night, some of the men in the lifeboat opened hatches when they saw the supply boat, and climbed out, hanging onto hand rails. When enough men did that, the lifeboat rolled over. On that black night, the supply boat crew could see the tiny strobe lights on the life jackets. Deck hands lashed themselves on the afterdeck, which was frequently totally awash, and tried to snag bodies with boat hooks as they washed on and off the deck. One by one, the little blinking strobes went out, killed by the same cold that killed the men wearing them.

Once again I have digressed, but the enormity of the personal tragedy for St. John still makes me pause. When the press tried to invade a community funeral service, they were almost tarred and feathered. I remember overhearing the press complain about that in the restaurant in the Marystown hotel, and I remember thinking the folks from Ottawa didn't know how lucky they were that they were only ushered out, their lights and cameras unwelcome guests for a grieving community.

Anyway, as we learned more, the list of immediate changes grew. On the 706, even though Barge Control was on the second floor of the quarters, we built steel shutters which could close off the windows. And more stuff like that.

One evening, passing through the hotel lobby, I heard a French accent asking for Jon LeBare. Somehow, it rang a bell, and I asked if he was looking for John Leber? He was, but he wouldn't tell me why, and insisted I follow him outside. He was a taxi driver.

He opened his trunk and there sat a large yellow cylinder, with radioactive markings and strict shipment prohibitions all over it. During a Type 4 inspection, certain critical welds are x-rayed for flaws. To x-ray, you must have a source of radiation. I was a little stunned, but it was that kind of time, a time of unusual methods and incredible hurry up. Someone had cut corners, but he was there safely.

He helped me load the thing (it was incredibly heavy for its size), into my rental car trunk. I slid and sloshed my way down the hill to the shipyard (the roads were snow on top of deep, deep ice, and driving was kind of fun---you had to drive like you were in a boat, not a car, and now that I understood front wheel drive, I used it to great benefit), and somehow got the thing out of my trunk by myself, and on to a little cart.

I got it to the Captain Ed, a little wooden harbor boat, and off to the 706 we went. I asked them to lower the personnel basket, but refused to tell them why on an open channel. A personnel basket is a conical net attached to a steel disk. Personnel put luggage and stuff inside the net, stand outside the net on the disk, hang on to the net, and get lifted by the crane up to the rig.

I decided that discretion was the better part of valor, and did not ride up with it. I figured the prominent black skull and crossbones would get it to the right people. I never heard a word about that late night delivery. It was just one more oddity in a time filled with oddities.

It was mid April before I returned to St. Johns. By then, all four sides of the rental had been dinged, dented, and clobbered, mostly while it sat in the hotel parking lot, I expect by the multitude of out of town drivers. The plastic thingy from under the engine was still in the back seat.

We were done, the rig was headed back to location. It was with great pleasure and secret glee that I dropped the keys on Jean's desk and asked her to return the rental. That, by the way, wasn't courage; I was on the way to the airport to leave the country, and I would probably be in the air before she saw the car.

Little did I know that that event would change the next few years of my life...

Regulatory nightmare—absolute safety

For the next several years I was sort of an "engineer without portfolio." I worked loosely 4 weeks on 4 off, although often it was more like 5 on and 3 off. My job was simply to deal with whatever things came up, and lots of things did.

I guess most people want to have an illusion of safety, to believe their world is dependable. Of course the world is not dependable, and none of us are truly safe. Offshore drilling is simply a little less safe than accounting or marketing. That's not to say it's not proper to maximize safety, it simply acknowledges that it's a dangerous business.

At one point the Province of Newfoundland was going to order the rigs to put 2 inch toe rails on all the walkways. A toe rail is a vertical edging along the walkway. The thought was that without toe rails, it was easy to kick something like a pipe wrench off and hurt someone. I got out the blueprints, and calculated the weight of 2 inches of ice on the walkways and its effect on vessel stability. It would make the vessel top heavy and prone to rolling over, and Newfoundland backed off toe rails.

There was great concern about icebergs. In fact, before the Ranger sank, icebergs were perceived to be the major threat. So one of the things we had to do was install a very expensive, super smart (for the time) radar unit. It had a nifty orange screen, and enough smarts to track and display the speed and course of things it saw.

Along with the new radar, we received new procedures. We had a yellow zone and an orange zone and a red zone, measured in distance from an iceberg was away from the rig, with specific steps to do if an iceberg entered each. That actually made sense, and formalized what had been informal procedures.

But being iceberg proof was a myth. One morning, the fog cleared, and sitting a half mile away, WAY inside the red zone, was an iceberg. The part that was out of the water was like a flat pyramid, which made it invisible to radar. In essence, it was a stealth iceberg. Radar waves hitting it would bounce out into space, not back to the radar.

While we frantically did all the yellow, orange, and red procedures, the iceberg very slowly moved directly away from us. It actually left the red zone before we could finish all of the red zone procedures. Icebergs are big enough they pretty much do what they want, ignoring procedures.

The industry learned from the Ocean Ranger. People, even engineers, cannot foresee every eventuality, and progress comes from learning as much or more than from wisdom. I said the Ranger trimmed down at the bow (tipped forward). Her pump rooms were in the aft (back end) of the pontoons. That meant that as she tipped, her pump rooms became higher than her forward tanks. Given her length, I think at about ten degrees trim she could no longer pump water out of the bow tanks.

You can only suck water up about thirty three feet. That's because you don't really suck water, you remove pressure on one side and air pressure pushes the water. It turns out air pressure equals the pressure of a column of water thirty three feet high, so even if you have a perfect pump, it can only pull water thirty three feet up.

You can, however, push water an almost unlimited distance. So another change Sedco made was to install submersible pumps inside the bow tanks. That way, no matter how tipped the rig was, the bow tanks could always be pumped out. I don't think of that as fixing an engineering error, I think of it as learning from experience.

We like to kid ourselves, pretend that we can make the world safe. But we can't. The trick is to understand that danger is all around us, always, and do what needs to be done anyway.

More on asking the right question

While in Brazil I went to out to a rig which was doing production (this means it was at a more or less permanent anchor, with hoses coming up from the ocean floor to a production plant which sent the oil produced to a waiting tanker). I went out to talk with the Barge Engineer about an upcoming annual inspection. The question I asked was whether or not we could de-ballast the rig high enough to do a dry inspection, and the answer was a resounding no.

During the underwater inspection, the cleaning divers came up and said they had found a crack. It turned out that they felt they had found a crack on a tubular member which wasn't even supposed to be inspected. However, I thanked them for their vigilance and assured them that the inspection divers would have a look, never believing for a second they had actually found a crack. The cracks looked for in an inspection are virtually never visible to the naked eye, and magnetic, sonic and other technologies are used to find defects.

To my great surprise, the inspection divers verified the existence of a crack. They took exact measurements and pinpointed the location. A flurry of telexes went back and forth between the naval architects in San Francisco, the engineering office in Dallas, and the rig office in Rio de Janeiro. In the meantime, the inspection crew proceeded on to a second rig.

When the second rig was finished a few weeks later, we had the inspection crew return to the first, just to be on the safe side. To everyone's absolute amazement, they reported measurable growth of the crack. This should have occurred in years, not weeks. The wires burned with telexes. The naval architects, in particular, were very excited. Could it be that the true design life of a rig had been reached?

There is a very good movie, "No Highway in the Sky", 1951 with James Stewart and Marlene Dietrich, which dealt with fatigue vibration failures in airplanes. Metal "fatigues" with vibration. Just as you can break a wire coat hanger by bending it a few times, the cyclic loading of a floating object by waves eventually will cause fatigue failures. To my knowledge, when "eventually" is for floating oil rigs is still unknown, but I believe that is partially why the naval architects were so interested. That, plus the fact that no one wants a vessel they designed to fall apart and sink.

The suggested short term fix was to drill two crack stopping holes. The idea behind that is that you drill a round hole at either end of the crack, and because the crack no longer has a sharp point, it cannot grow. Since the tubular with the crack was a nine foot diameter steel cylinder with one inch thick walls located about thirty feet underwater, I designed a drill harness which wrapped around the tubular and held the very large pneumatic drill steady.

The holes were drilled, but in a short period of time, a week or two, the crack jumped the holes and was continuing. Now the naval architects were in an absolute tizzy. It looked as if, in a fairly short period of time (meaning months or even weeks) the tubular could crack all the way around, at which point the rig would probably break apart and collapse into the sea.

All of which brings us back to the importance of asking the right question. Back to the Barge Engineer I went, only this time, the question was "what do we have to do to be able to bring the rig up, even including taking the derrick down, stopping production (a real "no no" in the eyes of our customer, Petrobras) and cutting the quarters apart and offloading them?

The Barge Engineer was a very pleasant fellow from England, and he and I cranked the numbers. The whole issue, as you bring a rig up, is that you must ensure it is not sufficiently top heavy that it falls over. Lo and behold, we could safely bring the rig up high enough to get the tubular a few feet above water level without much trouble, and without even stopping production. We got the blessing of Dallas engineering and the classification society, which for the rig involved was Lloyd's of London. I designed a simple open topped box to strap onto the tubular and protect the repair site from waves, and the rig welder built it.

A naval architect flew down from San Francisco and a properly certified welder flew out from somewhere. With the team on board, we began to bring the rig up. As the tubular began clearing the water the excitement was intense. It was a free flooding tubular, with open hatches on the top and the bottom. As it cleared the sea, the water drained out.

Once it had cleared the water, I opted to go in first, thankful for my training in marine biology. I had no idea what we would find, from sea snakes and nurse sharks that been caught unaware when their "cave" suddenly left the ocean to a dull and boring empty tube covered with barnacles.

It was exquisitely beautiful on the inside, with sponges still dripping sea water, corals of all colors, and sea urchins of many types. No higher life forms were still inside, which was a comforting disappointment. In a way it was too bad, by the end of the multi-day repair, the inside of the tubular was a dank, rotting, smelly bunch of indistinguishable dead stuff. But I am sure the ocean reclaimed the walls. In the ocean, hard surfaces are never wasted by the multitude of things which cling to something and sift the water for food.

Once inside, the source of the crack was clear. There was a very old defect, a gouge big enough to lay your finger in, probably dating back to a shipyard refit many years before. The crack on the outside was following the gouge, and almost certainly would have either totally stopped or drastically slowed down when it reached the limit of the internal defect, which it almost had already. Whether it was horribly sloppy work or intentional vandalism we'll never know.

The rest was tedium. The repair site had to be pre-heated, the crack and gouge cut out and filled, and the repair site then post heated according to the specs for that particular kind of steel. The naval architect and I spent many hours crouched in that steel box (about 5 feet long and 5 feet high) listening to the waves lap the tubular and making sure the heating pads, powered by welding leads running up to the rig's deck, never lost power or shorted out. I assume we chatted about family, work, and life, but I really don't remember.

On Remodeling

Did I mention that I was remodeling? It's not an experience I recommend. In fact, it's fortunate that I am no longer married; I can't imagine a marriage surviving remodeling. I want to divorce someone even though I'm not married!

The remodeling started with getting rid of the carpeting. With two big dogs, one cat, and sometimes two ferrets (they are in New York at the moment) pet hair is in abundance in my house. In the spring and fall the dogs track in dirt (and other nameless brown stuff) and while they are good dogs and totally house broken, they do have accidents, especially if they are sick.

Anyway, I decided the wall to wall carpeting had to go. Vinyl flooring with area rugs would be far easier to clean, I could carry coffee in the house with impunity, and it should drastically reduce dust. Little did I suspect the thought train was just beginning to move...

My kitchen has always been terribly short on storage space, and shares a common wall with the garage. Why not cut a huge hole in the wall, and build a pantry sticking out into the garage? My house was built with baseboard electric heaters which I have hated and routinely melted things like plastic clothes hampers (plastic hampers for clothes, to be precise).

Gee, if we're going to put in a furnace, maybe we can finally get gas from the gas company. Oh, and if we're paying for all the ducting for a furnace, central air only makes sense. But the windows are all old, falling apart, and very, very hard to clean.

As long as we're thinking about all that, the driveway is very old, sagging blacktop, hard to edge cleanly and a real eyesore. Cement would be clean, easy to shovel in winter, and easy to edge the grass in summer. But a clean, even, concrete driveway would kind of highlight the ugly depression in the front yard, where an ancient backfill apparently sank. Gosh, if we're going to fix the sunken spot, we really should get rid of the monstrous evergreen Danny, the kid across the street, broke 10 years ago and which is taking over the front of the house.

Putting in all new windows and flooring would make painting a snap. Let's repaint the whole inside of the house. As long as we're repainting, let's fix all the dings in the walls, patch the old holes, and finally fix the drywall where, years ago, I ran a separate circuit for the window AC.

That was all fine and good. But then I made the ultimate mistake. I decided to tackle my stuff! Looking back now, there was no dark sense of gloomy foreboding. With no hint of the terrible course I had chosen, I began to merrily lay plans, clueless to the terrible disaster I was walking into.

That was early November, and I sit writing this in mid-February. The daffodils I planted as part of the upgrade became confused by an unseasonably warm January, and are going to freeze their tushies off (do daffodils even have tushies??)

Anyway, my house is in shambles, my dogs are depressed and traumatized. My body aches and my feet smell bad. My garage is full of stuff, my living room is full of stuff, my old office is full of stuff, my basement is full of stuff, and I navigate my house staring at the floor to find a place to put a foot down without crushing stuff!

But again, I am getting ahead of myself.

More Stuff

*I*t *still amazes me how easily we can wander unwittingly into total chaos!*

Next we went to fill the depression in the front yard. It was a sunny, beautiful, Illinois fall day. A truck dumped a half ton of dirt on the center of the sunken spot, and we began spreading it and smoothing it with rakes, shovels, and high hopes. By the end of the day it was done, feathered into the rest of the lawn, and I was feeling so good I bought a package of daffodil bulbs (I think they were daffodils, the package at Lowe's had a picture of really pretty flowers on it....) and planted them in the fresh clean dirt along the edge of the house.

The next thing was a new driveway. It was great! A really nice young man dug up the old black top while I was in Chicago, and the next day he framed, poured, and smoothed the new one. Aside from parking in the street for a while, the improvements were proceeding without any schedule or life style disturbances. And, as long as I had to park in the street anyway, I moved most of the living room furniture into the garage, along with the furniture in the spare bedroom. That pretty much filled my one car garage.

The windows came and went in smoothly. With minimal moving of stuff, the old windows came out and the new vinyl ones went in. The furnace guy came and installed the furnace, ran all the ducting, piping, and gas lines to the outside. The gas company came and looked around for where to put the meter, and talked to the furnace guy (neither were named Bob, by the way).

This was going great!

My bathroom

My main floor bathroom measures 9 feet deep by 5 feet wide by 7' 9" high (call it 8 feet to make the math easy and the complaints better). That gives me two 9 X 8 walls, at 72 sq. feet each, or 144 sq. feet. Add in a 5 X 9 ceiling, another 45 sq. feet, and we now have 189 sq. feet. The front 5 X 8 wall is maybe half door, so call it 20 sq. feet, to bring us to 209 sq. feet. The back wall is mostly shower tub enclosure, so call it 8 square feet, getting us to 217 sq. feet. Round it up to 220, and I know how many square feet of paintable surface my bathroom has.

The paint was blistered and cracked, partly because I never cleaned the fan (nobody told me you needed to clean the fan) and the heat and moisture had worked their magic. We went to scrape off the loose paint, and chunks scraped off, leaving deep pits in the surface. I went to sand the remaining paint, and discovered the heat and moisture had transformed the paint that didn't fall off into a material almost certainly harder than diamonds. That was two weeks ago.

I sit here in my new brightly painted office trying to enjoy the bright late winter morning sunshine outside my new window. I cannot. Less than 10 feet away lurks my bathroom. My dogs slink past it on the far side of the hallway now. My hands on the keyboard as I type this still have paint, originally destined for the bathroom, testifying to my failures. My face is itchy with unshaven beard. I am sitting in part because my back hurts too much to do much else.

Nobody warned me about bathrooms, and let this serve as my warning to the world. Painting bathrooms is hell. It is that simple. Painting bathrooms is hell!

I suppose, for painters, this is a closely held trade secret. It must be relatively unknown because nobody told me! The bathroom is about half painted with the first coat of semi-gloss, but I am beginning to rethink the entire project. I have another bathroom, in great shape, in the basement.

Why does any house need two bathrooms? For that matter, my son and I are both named John, and our house has a bathroom in the basement and one upstairs. Why does any house need four johns?

The answer to both questions, of course, is that no house does! Already I feel better. I am going to get a new walk in closet!

My bathroom (soon to be closet) did teach me one thing, I'll admit. I took the wall mirror off early in the game, and put it on the floor of another room. I had the thought, bending over the mirror to comb bathroom debris out of what little hair I have left, that people who like to look down on other people should simply put a mirror on their floor.

Parkinsons and Mom and Dad

A few years ago my Mom was diagnosed with Parkinson's Disease. It was almost a relief, I had been suspicious of a series of small, undetected strokes to explain the loss of function. I sit here in the relative dark while the saxophone plays an upbeat melody, and am awed by my parents.

My parents have dealt with Mom's Parkinsons Disease the same way they have dealt with everything else, head on, with strength, determination, and love. They have moved into a condominium to eliminate yard work in the yard they loved, and are presently re-arranging the kitchen so Mom doesn't need to get things from high shelves. Mom is learning to use a computer, and Dad set up a spreadsheet for her to track her increasingly complicated medication schedule.

Mom can still carry a cup of coffee better than I can on most days, but the other day I scolded her for getting up on a footstool to reach a high shelf. I told her, in just so many words, that at her age all too often a broken hip is a death sentence. A woman who had no limitations must learn where and what they are now. Dad and Mom both seem to take special joy in the little happy things that happen daily, and support each other as best they can.

They were both recently at my house for a painting party, and Dad, at my request, primed the new window trim. Mom did what chores she could and made suggestions on process. Of course, she only made suggestions on process when her thoughts differed from mine. And of course, she was actually right the vast majority of the time, and while I don't like being wrong, I do enjoy doing a project the right way!

They are awesome, and they are truly, and totally, a "they." So many folks nowadays don't have the opportunity to be around elderly parents, and that is a shame. In much the same way that they were an adult roll model for me as a child, they are a roll model for me for the years to come. I have come to treasure my time with them, even if it's just for a cup of coffee in the afternoon.

Truth be told, I hope I will be up to the role model. I watch Mom walk through snow, carefully moving each foot, thinking about balance and each step. I am already paying a price for both doing many things I shouldn't have been able to do and for a sedentary life style the last 14 years. Mom just keeps doing the right thing and her best. Dad walks that line between respect and being too sympathetic, and hides pain and frustration and fear for her with patience and humor, or tries to.

Like I said, they are awesome.

The great motorcycle trip

Once in a while we make very good decisions, decisions that benefit us for a lifetime. I made such a decision in 1975. I had just finished Carleton College, and my brother Bill had just finished high school. It seemed to me that I would probably never again in life be that free of responsibilities and duties. So Bill and I decided to take a road trip by motorcycle.

At Carleton I had gotten quite good on a 10 speed bicycle, so I was confident that I could handle a motorcycle. Bill and I planned and prepared and bought stuff, professional quality stuff. We each bought a two man mountain tent, a down sleeping bag, a high quality backpack, and a Kawasaki 350 Enduro. The enduro part meant that it was basically a dirt bike but street legal. In essence, it was too big for dirt and too small for the road, but able to do both.

We packed and re-packed. Camera gear, fishing gear, camping gear. Clothes and personal items. Cold weather gear. Repair and 1st Aid gear. We bought a rear luggage rack and had a sissy bar welded on (a sissy bar is the high bar you sometimes see at the back of a bike, suitable for strapping on a backpack).

I give great credit to my folks in all this. It was a great adventure, and they were at least neutral, and often supportive. They never said, although they probably believed, "John, if you do this, you will come home in a box!" If my son were planning a similar adventure, I would have trouble being as strong as they were.

Finally we were ready. Our first stop—Granddad's farm in Southwestern Iowa, just north of Creston. We were only there for an overnight. As we were getting ready to leave, Grandpa told us, with a tiny smile, of the pioneers who dumped pianos in Missouri and silverware in Kansas. I think we felt smug, knowing we had trimmed to the bare minimum.

Then we were off. We avoided North Dakota because of Indian problems, and headed west through South Dakota. I remember just about dusk, somewhere in South Dakota, we pulled into a little diner for dinner. It was the first full day of living "on the road", and I felt so COOL! I was tired and dirty and dusty, and feeling a bit like Easy Rider [the movie with Henry Fonda's son].

We parked the bikes, took helmets off, and headed in. Actually, I expect I was swaggering in. I had only swaggered about 10 feet when I heard a huge crash behind me, and turned to find that the gravel under my kickstand had given way, and my bike had fallen over. The mood was shattered, and I moped my way back and stood the bike back up. For all I know, that little dose of reality early on saved my life. I was not Fonda, and this was not a movie.

In eastern Montana we met an honest to goodness cowboy mowing an Interstate Rest Stop. We offered him a drink of lemonade, and he stopped to chat a bit. He was old and a bit grizzled, and we told him we were from Illinois and out to see the West. He kind of chuckled, pushed his hat back a little, and told us that he had been east, been in New York and such places, and that the only reason that he could figure why folks lived east of the Mississippi "was cause they just didn't know any better!".

I think we were in Billings when we each mailed a box of unneeded stuff back home. I couldn't help but remember Granddad's words about stuff left on the prairie. We were usually camping in national forests, but once in a while, like in Billings, we would find an inexpensive motel and indulge in the luxury of things like running water.

It was a good life, being on the road. Time spent riding was solitary time. Time to enjoy the feel of the road and the bike, time spent in reflection or simple enjoyment of spectacular country. That time alone meant the time when we stopped, for gas or food or just to stop for a bit, was all the more special. Time to enjoy the easy company of a brother.

We headed south from Big Timber, Montana, for a lake on a mountain top in a national forest. Armed with topographic maps, advice from a local bike shop, and full tanks of gas, we expected to make camp before nightfall. We were wrong.

The gravel road turned to more of a path, winding up the valley. We found the horse trail that led up to the lakes and all was proceeding according to plan. It was riding my bike up the horse trails when I was rudely reminded that I have Cerebral Palsy.

The trail went up and down, sometimes rather steeply, and had gravel and rocks as a "surface." Some of the rocks were as large as six inches in diameter, so it was rough riding, worse going down, actually, than going up. We forded streams, climbed inclines so steep we had to put the backpacks on and stand up on the pedals, and slid down inclines with the rear wheel locked. Bill loved it, and was very good at it.

I really don't remember how many times I crashed and fell. Bill was very patient and not condescending at all. I think it was mid-afternoon when we were about half way there, instead of almost there. I bounced off a rock and, trying to stay upright, veered into a mountain meadow. It was a beautiful meadow, full of wildflowers. It was also full of small boulders, hidden in the grasses.

In no time at all I managed to stop my bike. It was lying on my leg, and the backpack was on my shoulders, and I was rather effectively pinned. So, while I waited for Bill to come help extricate me, I tried to enjoy the soft breeze of a Montana mountain in early summer. I failed. When he got there, I announced (with great restraint, I thought) "we are camping here!"

So we did. It was no big thing, we had water and food. We could finish the trip the next day. That night we talked it over by fire light. We were already a LONG way away from help if I were to break a leg or an arm. So, we agreed that the next morning I would chain my bike to a tree, and walk the rest of the way to the lakes, while Bill rode.

The next day that's what we did. Bill would ride ahead (a half mile, I think) and stop and wait for me. When I caught up, we would take a break and he would give me a Kraft caramel. In addition to regular camping stuff, my backpack had my motorcycle and fishing tools, my Nikon with three lenses and probably weighed in at 80 pounds or so.

It was well worth the walk. We camped by the lakes for a week. Every morning Bill would fish for trout, and every morning we would eat pancakes. The water in the lakes was clear, cold, and great tasting. During the days we would hike and explore, and I would take pictures. Wood was plentiful for a fire, the weather stayed beautiful, and life was good.

Motoring West

The trip back down the mountain was uneventful. On reaching Big Timber, we headed straight for a restaurant. I remember we both ate a big breakfast, and after eating for nearly an hour, decided to go ahead and order a lunch. The waitress was NOT pleased. I think she must have figured us for a flight risk. But even her glare couldn't dampen the sheer joy of eating a regular meal.

Bill had made friends at the local bike shop, and through them, we ended up getting jobs. It was my first time as an "engineer". Our job title was Geophone Placement Engineer. On the job, of course, we were called "juggies". We would shoulder a long cable with geophones every so many feet, and walk, uncoiling the cable as we went. When a geophone went down, we would stomp it into the ground. I think they kept me on the crew because Bill was so darn good at it, good equating to speed.

So we replenished our stake and moved on. We headed south through Wyoming and then into Colorado. In Colorado Bill decided that he needed to go seek his fortune, and he returned home. I headed west.

I found traveling alone to be in its own way satisfying. I had gone enough miles there was no fear, but there was a much greater feeling of "going somewhere" than before. I think in many ways wandering had been replaced by traveling, each with its own set of joys and tribulations.

Westward

Traveling alone, I found the lessons were different, ranging from the kindness of strangers to the stupidity of man...

Often, when I crossed a state line, I would celebrate by stopping for coffee. Utah was wide, hot, and straight. Interstate 80 just seem to stretch on forever. When I crossed into Nevada, I stopped at what I what I thought was a coffee shop, maybe it was.

Walking in from the outside in mid-day, I had to stop and let my eyes adjust to the darkness. I was expecting friendly hustle and bustle, a counter with truckers and maybe a buffet table in the middle of tables of travelers.

What I found was a dark place, full of noise and brightly colored lights. A little further in, I saw an old woman playing the slot machines. She looked like a machine. With absolutely no expression, she was playing three at once. Put in money, pull handle. Put in money, pull handle. Put in money, pull handle. By the time she had started the third, the first was done. I watched for a minute, and left.

I am sure that Nevada is a wonderful place, but I hurried across it and into California.

A professor of mine from Carleton was on Sabbatical at Berkeley, and I had had my juggie pay check mailed from Peoria to him. By the time I got close, I was just about out of money and very tired. As I neared the city, at night, I was lost and confused. I saw a green interstate street sign up a head, and thought "oh good, I'll find out where I am!" When I was close to read it, I was stunned. It said "A Street".

I thought to myself (expletives deleted), "I know it's a street, what street is it???" It wasn't until the next sign, a couple miles or so down the road, that I understood. The next sign said "B Street." I decided I was in no shape to cope with the city, rode back into the Golden Hills, and slept behind a huge (three or four stories high) pile of old tires.

The next morning, tired and nearly broke, I headed into San Francisco. San Francisco is a horrible city for a bike. The stop lights are all at the steepest part of the hill. A couple times I used the car stopped behind me as a backstop to get going when the light turned green.

At one point, on a fairly level street, at a stop light, I accidentally killed the bike while waiting for the light to change. I was so tired I wanted to just roll onto the sidewalk and sit down. Up next to me on my right pulled up a biker, a huge black guy on a huge Harley with a small jewelry store's worth of gold stuff on him. He made me a bit nervous.

He asked me if I'd ridden from Illinois, and I said I had. He just chuckled. I know he was thinking how ridiculously small my bike was for cross country travel.

After a moment of camaraderie, it was time to start my bike back up. I steeled myself, holding the clutch in and gripping the throttle tightly, and jumped up with my left foot, my right foot cocked to come down on the kick-start. I was so tired I didn't fire all the right muscles, and I went up, came down, but the kick-start didn't move, and I almost smashed my chin with my own knee. I told myself, "Right leg goes down, damn it!" Again I tried, and again my body refused. I was totally embarrassed, not to mention stuck immobile on that San Francisco street.

In the nicest possible way, the gentleman next to me asked if I could use a hand. Not knowing what he meant, I said yes. Still sitting on his huge bike, he reached his left foot across to my kick-start, and with no apparent effort at all, kick-started my bike for me. It was a little act of kindness that I've never forgotten.

It was also a reminder of how subtle and pervasive our own prejudices can be, even ones we strongly disapprove of.

On surgery

As parents, we pray our children won't make the same mistakes that we did, face the same trials, or take the same risks. I certainly hope my son won't opt to cross country tour on a motorcycle! And yet, at the same time, we must realize they will face their own challenges, and there is nothing that we can do about it.

When he finished fourth grade, son John was invited to attend a gifted program, 5th through 8th. I was very proud of him, of course, but a little ambivalent about the invitation, having spent many years pushing for full inclusion of all students. The gifted program allowed 60 students each year from all over the city, and kids were bused to the "gifted school." The final decision whether to leave his neighborhood school was left up to him.

We didn't know it at the time, but when he walked in the door at the start of 5th grade, he had Lymphocyte Predominant Hodgkins Disease, a form of cancer. That summer, our pediatrician had retired (he had been my pediatrician decades before), so we had a new one by referral.

Daughter Sally was having all kinds of physical complaints, from headaches to dizziness to sore muscles, and it was largely with her in mind that I scheduled two "get acquainted" visits with the new guy. In Sally's case, the morning of our afternoon appointment, I took in a written list of concerns I wanted the doctor to know about but didn't want to tell him in front of Sally. At the bottom of that list, I confessed that I truly couldn't tell what was real and what might not be when it came to headaches and such.

A little while before the appointment for John, he told his mom he had noticed a lump in his upper cheek, and she told me. I didn't think a great deal about it, but mentioned it to the pediatrician. I was surprised how quickly we had an appointment with a surgeon, an Eye/Ear/Nose/Throat guy who was also a plastic or cosmetic surgeon. The initial diagnosis was a benign parotid tumor, or a swelled up tear gland.

Mr. H, a long term friend of my family, dating back to when I was a baby, was there with John's mom and I during surgery. He and John's mom had stepped out of the waiting room when the surgeon zipped out. He hurriedly told me it wasn't a parotid gland, it was a lymph gland, and they had sent it for biopsy. Then he hurried off. Other than vague feelings of misgivings, I didn't think a lot about it. My focus was on John right then.

That evening, in the hospital, folks came and went, subject to the splits and schisms in the family (by this time John's mom was living in a small town 20 miles west of Peoria). John's mom didn't want to see my folks, so when they came, bringing my daughter Sally, John's mom had absented herself.

John tried to eat a dinner. Getting rid of the IV was dependent on being able to take nourishment and liquids the regular way. He really only managed the red jello, probably cherry.

The folks left with Sally, and John and I were alone. I knew he felt very badly; he didn't have the energy or interest to play the Nintendo provided in the room. Out of somewhat of a daze, John said to me "I'm going to be sick."

I grabbed a big white towel as the first thing I could find as John sat up. He threw up into the towel. I thought, hoping it didn't show, "My God, it's blood!" Holding him, my heart pounding, telling him it was ok (he was embarrassed), I found and pressed the emergency call button.

In almost no time a nurse showed up, and she looked as concerned as I was, as John continued to soak a towel bright red. Suddenly it hit me, and I looked at the nurse and said "He ate red jello!" She seemed as relieved as I was. She and I never discussed that 30 or 60 or however many intense seconds. I believe we both thought something had "let go" inside of John.

For my money, hospitals should NEVER serve red jello to anyone, ever. Red jello should be banned from medical buildings. Possession of red jello inside a hospital should be a Class 1 Felony! Fortunately, that was years ago, and I no longer feel quite so strongly about the issue of red jello in hospitals. I no longer want to kill someone!

Anyway.....

John's mom spent the night at the hospital with him and the next day I was able to take him home. The IV was gone but he had this huge bandage thingy on his head. No one at the hospital had really told me what it was for, what to do if it came off, or anything about it.

For hours, that first night, we struggled with it. It didn't want to stay put. It was uncomfortable. It leaked blood. By 4 in the morning I was beside myself. There is no feeling on earth worse than not knowing how to help your child.

I called the hospital but couldn't find anyone who knew anything about John. The last thing I wanted to do was force John to get up and go with me to the emergency room, especially if it was totally unnecessary. John finally dozed off.

I hopped on AOL, and did a member search for anyone who was online with the occupation nurse. I picked one, and sent an Instant Message, apologizing for intruding and asking for help. I explained the situation, and she explained that the thing on his head almost certainly was a protector for a drain tube running back from the place of surgery to behind his ear.

Once I understood the concept, the worry over the unknown was gone. It was not a medical emergency, it was simply a matter of mechanics to get the "thing" on his head to stay put. I took gauze and made him a turban while he slept. I watched him sleep for a while, and finally grabbed a blanket and curled up on his floor.

As I think about those two days, several things impress me. The first is the power of the human mind. At least for me, in some situations walls slam down, like emotional flood control. I do not believe John ever knew how afraid I was. For that tiny window of time in the hospital, I thought he might be dying in front of my eyes. Hours later, talking to my friend in Spokane by cell phone from the hospital parking deck, I cried like a baby.

The second thing that impresses me is the power of information. With the exceptions of sub-atomic physics and electronic engineering, there is nothing I know of which cannot be put in plain English. Sub-atomic physics borders, in language, on Zen mysticism, and electronic engineering uses the square root of negative one, which in the world I live in is an impossibility. Other than those two, all things I know about are common sense plus information.

Cancer

It is amazing how perspective can change in an instant. Everything that was important can suddenly seem trivial. There is a lesson in that, a lesson best learned from words, not experience. At least I certainly don't recommend the experience.

The surgeon who did the operation is, I expect, a very good surgeon. His people skills could use work, though. We got John's biopsy results when we went in to have the stitches removed. It was in the surgeon's office, an outpatient building. He called us into the hall, just outside the door to the room John was in.

John's mom and I stood there, still in winter coats, between the nurses' station and John's door, and he told us that John had Hodgkin's Disease. I think John's mom heard a death sentence, and she fell apart. Not knowing what else to do, I held her for a few moments, and looking over her shoulder, asked a nurse if there was someplace she could sit down. The nurse took us to an unused examination room, and once she was sitting, I hurried back to John, not knowing what he had heard.

I was afraid he had heard his mother's cry of anguish and tears, but he hadn't. So we talked about a bunch of nothing, and I think I told him he could blow off school for the rest of the day. His mom rejoined us, and I think I suggested they go to lunch. After I watched them drive off, I sat in the parking lot and lost it. I just sat there in my car, feeling furious and helpless and so afraid, and cried. I called my folks by cell phone, conveyed the information, and ended the call before I lost it again.

I had to do something! Anything constructive. I had to. So I drove to the school and asked for a private conference with the principal, a very efficient and stern but very nice lady. The kind of lady whose huge heart can sometimes appear hidden by tough love, if the situation demands it.

I don't think I cried in her office, but I wouldn't swear to it. I told her John didn't even know yet, and she promised to work with us to help John however they could. She asked for permission to tell his teachers, and I agreed.

Sitting here now, writing this, I know walls slam down. I can feel the un-shed tears, even though all is well now. My dogs are hanging close again...

St Jude

*P*eoria *has the first St. Jude affiliate outside of Memphis. Mayor Maloof, long retired now, was friends with fellow Lebanese Danny Thomas, and he and Doctor Hart (my pediatrician) formed the St. Jude Midwest Affiliate. After the biopsy was analyzed in Peoria, it was automatically shipped to Memphis for confirmation.*

Our first appointment with St. Jude was on a Friday afternoon. John's mom and I went in with John. I was really expecting a get acquainted meeting, I guess. I think I also was expecting a grim place, constantly battling cancer to save children. Boy was I wrong!

Before we left that Friday, we had a battery of tests scheduled in Memphis for the following Monday, $70 in cash for gas, and instructions to get our hotel coupons at St. Jude hospital in Memphis when we arrived Sunday night. And the kids who were there, infants through teenagers, were playing Nintendo, doing crafts, and generally having a ball, kidding and joking with staff.

I was struck by so many things at once in Memphis. St. Jude is an incredible place: laid back yet extremely professional; friendly and bright and fun and battling the death of children; prestigious and huge and down home. St. Jude embraced us, and our problem was theirs.

I was initially horrified by the number of amputees-kids missing parts. In the Civil War, ok, if you couldn't cure, you cut. But my god, this is now.

Many forms of cancer aren't yet curable. So if you can't cure, you still cut. The scientist/engineer in me rebelled at our lack of knowledge. We can put a bomb dropped from 30,000 feet into a 10X10 foot hole, but we don't have a cure for kids with cancer.

We spoke, while we waited once, with a 15 year old boy, who talked matter-of-factly about dying before he had made love. He had a particularly vicious kind of leukemia, is probably dead now, and probably did die without ever making love. Sitting here now, in the "real" world, it's almost impossible to capture the mixture of hope and love and peace at St. Jude. It doesn't seem possible, given the nature of the task they've tackled.

Every single time John had a test, he got to pick a toy. An X-Ray, pick a toy. A CAT Scan, pick a toy. An MRI, pick a toy. St.

Jude has red wagons, bright red wagons. The kind of wagons used to roll crazily down a grassy hill on a summer day. Only at St. Jude, they carry infants and toddlers, surrounded by toys and love, through the antiseptic, brightly painted hallways.

St. Jude is medicine practiced the way it should be practiced, family centric medicine, priceless medicine. Not priceless in the sense of expensive, priceless in the sense of without price, like the kids they try and help. The kids they do help, even the ones they lose.

The courage and love of the staff at St. Jude are totally immeasurable. It's incredible. John is healthy and well and now a teenager (we'll get through that, too). If it wasn't for the work and research of St. Jude, he would probably be dead. There are no words to convey the gratitude I feel, no words at all.

2nd year

Sometimes uncertainty can be more difficult to deal with than the worst "real" problem. I think fear of doing the wrong thing for a child may be the worst fear of all.

It was John's second time in fifth grade that getting him to school became a problem. 4 out of 5 days I would end up taking his temperature before telling him to get up and go to school. For years I had given sage advice to parents of kids with disabilities about walking the line between codling and understanding, between crippling with pity and building with respect and rules, yet I was clueless with my own son, navigating in the dark.

One morning, he just wouldn't get out of bed, but he had no temperature. I manhandled him out of bed and got him dressed and upstairs to the couch. An extra stress was a meeting that I absolutely had to be at that morning. I grabbed him by the upper arms and stood him up. He said to me, in an absolutely baby, tiny voice, "Don't hurt me."

Something broke inside. I held him and hugged him and we sank to the floor. I sat there and cried and rocked him. But I did absolutely have to go.

So I called my Mom, and I asked her, "Take John to the pediatrician and test for absolutely EVERYTHING. I need to know there is nothing wrong before I act on the psychologist's recommendation to be tough with him."

So she did. It turned out one kind of blood test they couldn't do at the pediatricians. There were only three places in town that could do it.

One of the three was where he had gotten blood tests and chemotherapy for six months. His mom would hold him and he would bury his head and he would go into shock. He had developed a totally understandable aversion to needles of any kind.

I was done with the appointment by then, but I told my Mom on the phone,, "any place but the chemo lab, and I don't want to be there." And I asked her, "please don't call his Mom". She understood completely, there was to be no connection with the settings or people where drawing blood had been so difficult.

She took him to an outpatient lab, and they took the blood. He did not go into shock; did not have trauma. He even said, when it was done, "that wasn't so bad."

In that time, I clung to small victories of any kind. Before then, all through my life, I had never understood the term "breakdown." I just didn't get it. Now, I think, I have been close enough to total overload that I can at least empathize a little.

It is an agonizing line to walk, that line between sympathy and pity. Sympathy, in the right situation, can help. Pity always cripples. But it is an unclear line, shifting and blurry. You just have to take your best shot, I guess.

Strange as it may sound, I was overjoyed to learn he had mononucleosis. And I could be free to spoil and pamper him for a couple of weeks. A break for both of us!

Snorkel man and Liz

It is amazing how much of a person can come across a digital stream, likes and dislikes, humor and patience or lack thereof.

Across five or six years, once in a while I would visit an AOL "chat room". Not any particular room, I just accepted where the system put me (I would pick Divorced Only in category Romance, and the system would tell me it was full, and offer to put me in Divorced Only 25, or 10, or something). Once in a while it was fun, most often it was boring because I was an "outsider", kind of like my marriage.

During that time I gained a sister. I had never had a sister, only two brothers. Liz is a delightful, wonderful, and lovely woman in Ecuador. I have been talking to her for 7 or 8 years, and she helped me through my son's cancer, my divorce, emotional upheavals, and the roller coaster that I call my life of late.

She still sometimes refers to me as Snorkel Man, because I told her, early on, of a trip to Key Largo when I was living in Ft. Lauderdale. I have always required eyeglasses to drive, being moderately near sighted. So I was very concerned when I broke my glasses in Key Largo. I broke one ear piece off, and no matter what I did with string and rubber bands, couldn't seem to make them stay on.

Then I remembered. I had my diving mask in the car, and it had prescription lenses. So it was that I drove from Key Largo to Ft. Lauderdale in my diving mask. And since that meant I had to breathe through my mouth, I used the snorkel just for fun.

If you happen to see a strange person driving down the road in a diving mask, be slow to judge. There may be a perfectly good explanation. Of course, they might just be masking other problems...(I did say low humor).

Pay Attention

Ted died from AIDS while I was in Brazil, and I didn't learn about it until much later. He contracted HIV while sharing a needle with a friend. I have thought about Ted a lot, and pondered life's vagaries. In many ways, if there ever was a man who accomplished the goals life gave him, it is Ted, even though his life was shorter than most.

Allegedly, Ted had been a junky in Massachusetts as a young man, and a judge had given him a choice: the Army or jail. He chose the Army. He ended up a Drill Instructor, I believe. That's about all I know about the early days.

By the time I got to know him, his wildest days were past. When I first got to know him, he was still hustling. Ted, for me, is more a memory of the feeling of a man than specifics. He was a man who was an untamed power. He was a man of simple and sometimes violent rules.

But most of all, he was fundamentally a good man. His heart was big and good. The world had forged a hard man, a strong and sometimes ruthless man, but his heart was good. His heart was huge. By the time he died, he was a boat broker, not a hustler. By the time he died, he was a good husband. By the time he died, he was a member of a church.

The pastor asked him, before he died, what advice he would give to others. His answer? Simply "Pay attention!" Those who loved him honored his wishes, and the last time he went into arrest they did not call 911 until they were sure he was gone, his physical power in our world destroyed by AIDS.

His was the kind of power and loyalty which makes me imagine myself at the gates of Heaven, being turned down, and hearing his voice from behind the gatekeeper, saying "Excuse me!!!"

I still wish I had told him how special he was.

Unloading chopper first hitch

I have come to value experience greatly. Not only can it make something far easier, in some cases it can save your life. The trick sometimes is living long enough to gain it.

There was a rig medic, Leroy, who probably saved my life years ago. It was my first hitch, and I was on the maintenance crew. One of our jobs was to unload the helicopters when they landed. I think I had been on board only a day or two when I went up to help unload my first, a Sikorsky 61, I think. Our hardhats were strapped on, and the noise was deafening. The choppers never shut down, they just idled while unloading and loading.

The chopper crew were handing out things, and most guys got pieces of luggage belonging to incoming crew and took off toward the quarters walkway. I was given a big cardboard box, and when I turned to follow the others, the warehouseman intercepted me and pointed toward the aft of the chopper. It is hard to explain how noise and wind can almost shut down the mind, without experience and training. I started walking the way he had pointed, eyes on the helideck so the netting didn't trip me, almost overwhelmed by the magnitude of sensory input.

Suddenly, I was grabbed from behind by Leroy, the medic, who had come up behind me at a run. He spun and swung me around and away from the chopper. He pointed, and I realized I had been walking right at the tail rotor. I yelled (talk was impossible), that the warehouseman had told me to go that way, and Leroy yelled back that the warehouseman meant go way around but end up at the warehouse.

For me, it was an object lesson in the value of training and experience. Working around choppers and cranes and huge diesel engines became commonplace for me. Even noise so loud it rattles your fillings can be filtered out and ignored by the mind. But, at least for me, that was a learned ability, not an inherent one.

I think the mind can learn filters, or mechanisms for coping, for almost any environment, but it is foolish arrogance to assume we already have them for all situations. I will say, though, the broader the base of experience an individual has, the more quickly he can adapt to new situations. If strategies have been learned for a similar situation, adapting to a new one is easier and faster.

That is the value of experience. Unfortunately, I have yet to find any method for instilling appreciation of experience into teenagers. I sometimes think that they simply haven't made enough mistakes to appreciate the wisdom of those who have made many more.

Freedom (a continual fight)

A few years ago I had an opportunity to testify before an Illinois Senate committee hearing testimony about community services for individuals with disabilities. It was my first time testifying, and they wanted a written copy of any testimony given. I was next to the last of maybe 20 people, and was there, in part, as Vice President of UCP of Illinois.

That was one of the many times in my life when I blew it. Testimony given before mine included testimony from a grand old matriarch of residential services, a very politically powerful woman who no doubt believes very strongly in her services, which are not community based. In her testimony, she related that her agency had placed people in the community, but on follow up visits, found that they were lonely, distressed, and without friends, and they took them back into the institution.

Finally, my turn to testify came, and I stuck to my written, prepared testimony. I was horribly nervous, and it showed. I talked about dry economic benefits to the taxpayer of community based services. It was only in the car, on the three hour trip back from Chicago, that I said what I should have said in the hearing.

Sitting in my car on I-55, I reviewed the afternoon. By the time I reached I-80, I knew what I should have said:

Honorable Senators:

My name is John Leber, and I am from Peoria. I do appreciate this opportunity to testify, and have submitted written testimony concerning the economic benefits of serving the developmentally disabled in community, rather than institutional, settings. I now must address some testimony you have heard earlier.

I have a disability, and use assistive technology to be able to operate a motor vehicle. I must wear eye glasses to drive. I also have a developmental disability, Cerebral Palsy. I am self employed and spend large amounts of time working alone. I am occasionally lonely. I have a teenage daughter and son, so I am occasionally distressed.

Heaven help the individual, or the institution, or the government which shows up on MY front porch and says "John, you are lonely. You are distressed. So we will TAKE you and GIVE you community and GIVE you friends."

I know, Senators, that their intent may be honorable. But while they are GIVING you these things, like a thief in the night they are STEALING your life!

That is what I should have said. Maybe saying it here is a catharsis. Or maybe the words, once thought, just had to find a way to get out.

FAU housing

The last few years I was at Florida Atlantic University I lived in a variety of settings, some interesting, some peculiar, and all temporary. At one point I lived right on the beach in a very expensive area of Boca Raton. The apartment had been vacated by the sister of a gal who worked for me on and off. The sister had gone to Las Vegas with get rich quick schemes involving drugs, and ended up murdered in the desert. But that is another story.

We were a rag tag bunch of renters in an ancient building the owner was keeping until someone met his price for the property. The building was run by a tenant/super who collected rent as part of his rent, an aspiring author of mystery books. We were all riff raff, more or less.

I had only been there a month or so when an eviction notice showed up on everyone's door, served on October 8th, each with a backdated, personalized letter of notification. No one had actually received the letter in the mail, and I don't believe they were ever sent. Someone was just in a hurry to tear the building down.

I was truly annoyed. They (whoever they were) had, in my opinion, started a legal action against me with falsified evidence, and were just assuming I would vanish, which is what all the other renters did. And so it was I pulled out the Smith Corona and dusted it off.

If this were an action movie, this is the scene where the hero straps on knives, loads and holsters guns, and snaps the slide on the shotgun to chamber a shell. In this case, the camera zooms in the typewriter keys as they are dusted, closes in on the paper as it is loaded, and the scene ends with the resounding clap as the bar snaps down on the paper (Younger readers may have absolutely no idea what that might look like---trust me, it would be an impressive scene).

I drove to the county court house and picked up a copy of the complaint. I read carefully through the legalese, and apparently doing nothing was agreeing to the claims in the complaint. However, responding did not require a lawyer. It simply required a written response to the lawyer, filed with the court, which would generate a court date for a hearing.

So, tap tap tap, tap, typing on into the night. Finally, I was done. I had the response.

The response borrowed legalese from the eviction. I had until October 13th to file written response. I remember thinking, "what the heck, it's kitchen sink time", and I added a kind of cover letter to the October 9th letter.

The cover letter referenced the worry, stress, and, of course, the difficulty of moving on short notice with Cerebral Palsy (total bunk in my case). I wrote it to look like I was intending to sue, which I wasn't.

I remember how perplexed the secretary looked at the prestigious law firm when I dropped it off. I obviously wasn't a lawyer nor a courier, and certainly not a client. My long hair and rough clothing were totally out of place in the plush office. She was quite nice though, and agreed to sign and date a copy I had brought along for that purpose. I dropped a copy off to the court too, both on October 13th, the fifth and final day for filing an answer.

On October 20th the Palm Beach County Court set a final hearing date for October 29th, with all parties ordered to be present. On October 24th, the lawyer for the owners threw in the towel completely, filing a "Voluntary Dismissal Without Prejudice", legalese for "oops, never mind." I was ecstatic, and I felt like filing a notch in my typewriter!

Of course, by then I was living in a KOA campground and showering at the school's gymnasium.

It is interesting to me how much is done in this country by companies and people who just expect to get away with it because of an assumption that those from lower educational or economic levels will let them. I wish schools could put more self advocacy training into the general curriculum. Of course, schools might not want to create a student body full of self advocates....

Children (a composite)

Once in a while a moment is so perfect that you just have to try and capture it, if only by paying attention...

07/28/97

Weather broken, sitting on front porch with Sally. Black birds beginning to gather, just sunset now. Maybe a hundred in a favorite tree provide constant backdrop of chatter. Nine kids, both of mine, dancing under a tree across the street to a boom box playing SpaceJam. Two tiny kids gyrating in my front yard.

Just enough wind to keep bugs away. Rap now. They're all just jumping up and down. High cirrus clouds turning orange on a sky of deepening blue.

All but clouds in shade now. Twilight feeders, nighthawks, putting on an aerobatics show.

Clouds now pink and purple cotton candy. Music gone, kid noises carry on the wind.

A quiet summer night

Children at peace

It's 10:30 in the evening, and shadows move and laugh on a driveway across the street. The night is dark and clear, just a half moon in the high west, the Big Dipper high overhead. It's past bed time, and the voices and laughter are hushed and excited. A group collectively "getting away with something."

It's a cool clear night, a refreshing change from the oppressive heat of a few days before. Son John asks for permission to play monopoly inside a neighbor's house, and, after a brief negotiation, it's agreed, the end of the game or midnight, which ever comes first. Cowboy ballads quietly add the background noise, and I turn to write this and remember quiet summer nights decades ago, much the same.

An hour later and it's "Ghost in the Graveyard", a chasing game in the dark. I sit on the porch in the dark and listen and smile, remembering, enjoying their pleasure. No music now save the squeals of delight and excitement. Very soon it will be tomorrow. He'll sleep soundly tonight!

A focus on now is a child's blessing.

07/01/1998

I think there is a lot we could learn from young children if we only paid attention. The love I have for my children just does not fit into words.

New Orleans with a 357 magnum

Years ago I flew from Belize to New Orleans after a vacation with Larry, my college roommate from Carleton. We had gone to Belize to camp and snorkel and hang out. Since we had planned on camping in the jungle, I took along a Dan Wesson 357 handgun I had purchased in Florida for doing security guard work.

I reached customs with my framed backpack in a weathered straw cowboy hat, jeans, and a denim cowboy shirt, the kind with pearl (well, fake pearl) snaps instead of buttons. The 357 was broken down, unloaded, and locked in a small steel chest. I handed the lady the key and told her the chest contained a hand gun.

In no time at all two men in suits, with white shirts and thin black ties, showed up and invited me to the "back room." I had a three hour layover, so I was in no hurry. They politely flanked me as we walked back to an inner office.

For the next half hour or more we danced a dance of definitions. They were polite, but unfriendly, wanting to define me as a suspect. I was polite and friendly, defining them as public employees, and as such, working for me. They would ask "Did you go to any other country?" and I would say "No, I sure didn't" and inquire about restaurants in the airport, explaining that I had a long layover.

After a bit and after examining the weapon, the younger one left, while the older one and I continued the dance. After a while, and toward the end of our visit, the younger one returned and announced, rather imperiously, that he had run the Smith & Wesson serial number, and it was clean, and I was free to go. I immediately looked concerned. I carefully and politely explained that Dan Wesson was a lesser known manufacturer, but completely different from Smith & Wesson (something about Wesson must get families into weapons…hmmm, oils too, the vegetable kind….I don't know), and I said he needed to go and run the serial number with the proper manufacturer.

To their credit, he did exactly that. While he was gone, the older one gave up, and I didn't push it, so we sat mostly in silence. The dance was done.

I figured it was it a good trade. They helped me kill some time between flights, and I taught them something they really should have known. At least, that's how I like to think about it.

Sally and the "position of function"

My daughter Sally was born in Dover, NH, and I was able to be there. For reasons I don't recall, she was born by Caesarian delivery, so I never used the Lamaze class I took with my wife. Which is ok, if looks could kill, the Lamaze class teacher would have killed me when I told her that I might not be around. At that time I was still working in Newfoundland a month at a time, and my being there wasn't my call.

Anyway, it went fine and they whisked her away. Some of this comes from my Mom's memory, I think because I blocked it out. When I looked through the glass at my daughter, she had casts on both feet with a steel bar going from cast to cast. I had no idea why.

I tried to find out, but no one would tell me. I went to see her mom, who was still doped up from surgery, and she assured me everything must be fine. But I knew everything wasn't fine! It looked like my firstborn was trussed up in some kind of medieval torture apparatus.

Years before I had listened to a pediatric orthopedist talking at a conference about the "position of function." He spoke with the sad wisdom of 20/20 hindsight. There had been a school of thought that if you could force the hands of an individual with Cerebral Palsy into a "normal" position, it would help with function. So a bunch of very small children were functionally tortured, their hands strapped into a "normal" position and their muscles shocked electrically so the hands would stay in that position. It didn't work, and actually made things worse.

That was the only thing I could think of, and no one would talk to me! I was frantic. I thought about grabbing my daughter and absconding to another hospital. I actually thought about doing that at gunpoint if necessary, I was that upset and worried.

Then I saw the doctor in the hallway. I think I got in front of him and grabbed his lab coat. I explained my concern and why, and demanded to know why my daughter was constrained. My guess is that he realized he was very close to being seriously hurt if he didn't talk to me, and suddenly I had a caring, sharing physician. Or, more charitably, he realized how distraught I was, I don't know.

It turned out that Sally was born with bilateral club feet, and the casts and bar were correct treatment. Why no one would tell me until I nearly went "postal" I'll never know. I believe, and hope, that the medical profession is far better about communication now, and the concept of "doctor as God" has been beaten back by public outrage and medical schools' adjustment of curricula and style.

On Malted Milk Shakes

I decided long ago that simple pleasures are important. Being a connoisseur of fine wines is fine, I suppose, especially if you can afford fine wines. Clearing the palate, swirling the glass, sniffing, tasting with an elegant sip, little finger out of course, all of that pales compared to the knowledge it takes to properly enjoy a malted milk shake.

The best malted milk shakes in the world were made in Newcomb's drug store until they went out of business, years and years ago. Newcomb's was in Creston, IA, on the corner of First and Main, had five stools at a counter that still had a full size Marilyn Monroe card board cutout behind it, and a cigarette bin made by Lucky Strike up on the wall.

They used the institution green stirring machines with two stirring places, real malt, and hand scooped ice cream. The next best thing is a Steak & Shake Malt, still available today. A "small" Steak & Shake malted milk shake comes in a glass the size of a large iced tea glass in a family restaurant. The glass is a glass glass, not plastic, and well chilled before use. When the malted arrives at your table, a cherry sits atop a flower of whipped cream, about an inch above the sides of the glass.

There are probably as many ways to proceed as there are malted aficionados. What follows is simply one of many techniques.

1) Very slowly slide the straw down through a high point in the whipped cream, missing the cherry. You may note that by the time the straw is one inch into the malted, it is stable, and may be released, if desired. The malted is sufficiently thick the straw will no longer fall, although with only an inch in the malted, it may slowly tip sideways. Sliding the straw all the way to the bottom of glass, however, will stabilize both it and the whipped cream.

2) Using the long handled spoon provided, carefully lift the cherry from the whipped cream, with however much whipped cream and malted as desired to sweeten and flavor the cherry.

3) By this time, the frosted glass will have condensed enough that a careful examination of the malted is possible through the sides of glass. It is uniform, and sufficiently thick that bubbles with diameters of up to a millimeter or more can be observed suspended in the glass. Using the spoon, enjoy the whipped cream with as much malted as desired for flavoring.

4) Now it is time for the malted, an exquisite experience of sensory enjoyment. The straw should not be raised from the glass, the glass and straw should be raised to the lips. This allows the layering of whipped cream within straw to remain intact. Sucking slowly on the straw, note the delicious change from whipped cream to malted as the top inch in the straw is consumed.

5) Two methods are worth mention concerning consumption of the malted itself. The first is to secure the straw by hand, which is probably easier for the novice. The second is to roll the tongue around the straw, pressing it gently against the upper teeth to hold it secure. The latter method is referred as hands free, and is generally preferred by experienced suckers. In both methods, however, the necessity of not sucking too quickly is paramount. If the mouth is chilled too thoroughly, taste can be lost. As a general rule of thumb, three sucks to six breaths is considered conservative and appropriate.

As a final note, the straw is NEVER used to stir, disturb, or otherwise damage the integrity of the malted. This is an obvious indication of a rank amateur, who should probably have gone to a drive through fast food place!

On spelunking and golf

M_y *Junior year at Carleton College, located in Northfield Minnesota, I was privileged to spend one ten week term at the Bermuda Biological Station along with 22 other biology majors. Also at the station at the same time was a geologist named Michael, who happened to be a world class spelunker. He had the equipment and the knowledge, and found a willing pool of volunteers in the Carleton students—some of us anyway.*

Bermuda in winter is cool. It's also relatively inexpensive, so our biology seminar there started in January. It was wet suit diving and it seemed that we were the only ones using the beaches. Bermuda, with its British heritage, is an extremely civilized place, and we were a bunch of rag tag yanks bopping about doing silly things like body surfing in February. One of the things civilized folks can do in wintertime in Bermuda, though, is golf.

The fact that the golf courses had golfers is the reason we went caving at night. I don't know how Michael knew where they were, but the caves we explored had entrances in the overgrown woods along the fairways. It was spectacular. We actually got to places no one had ever gotten too, and in one case, left our foot prints in a 10,000 year old untouched talus slope.

While none of the rooms were huge, some were the size of a small hotel room, and when we reached water, it was so clear and so still the surface was a foot or two above where you thought it was. On one of these trips, we got back to surface a little after dawn.

I was the first one out, and took off my helmet and light and set them down. The cave entrance was a few yards up a densely wooded hill from a fairway. That particular cave was accessed by making a 10 or 15 foot belly crawl along a muddy wet tube. I had on a denim shirt and jeans, but was mostly the color of mud by then.

Well, I went to pick up my helmet and tripped. Trying to run my feet back under me, I ran downhill, burst out of the thick brush, and sprawled face down sliding onto the fairway. That was no big thing. It was a gorgeous morning, bright sun making the dew on the manicured fairways glisten and shine. I stood up, admiring the view, and feeling thankful that none of my fellow students had seen my antics.

I turned to go back into the brush and saw them. About ten feet away were two impeccably dressed golfers, British I think. Golfing shoes, crispy white socks, light colored shorts, and, of course, polo shirts. They were standing absolutely still, hands still on their little pull carts for their golf bags, just staring at me. For a few seconds I stared back, brushing the dirt off the front of my shirt, my mind a blank. Finally, I asked "Have you seen a Titlelist 9?"

We all stood stock still, with no expression. I let my eyes shift from one to the other. Finally, the one on the right said "Sorry, no."

I tried my best to produce a rueful smile, and trudged back up into the dense brush and forest edging the fairway.

To this day I wonder if there aren't two Brits still talking about the crazy Yank looking through dense jungle for a golf ball in Bermuda, as they sit in a posh London club.

On aging

I guess I am satisfied with the first half century, neither extremely proud, nor very distraught with the way it went. Lots of successes and some very notable failures are spotted across the decades. But all in all I am satisfied.

I am comfortable with who I am but not what I am doing, but that is a never ending process. I believe we are all (or should be) works in progress. The remodeling job has reminded me how much I enjoy working with wood, varnishing and painting and smoothing and shaping. I need to do more of that; in fact, I need to do more of all of the things I enjoy.

I am aware of many mistakes, and try to learn from them without basking in guilt. I enjoy the many good memories of people and places. At the same time I do not consider myself remotely done making good memories, and I am sure, mistakes to learn from.

I am old enough to notice aging. Cerebral Palsy exacerbates aging, no one knows why. In my opinion, it is simply a matter of paying dues for wear and tear, and losing abilities that were marginal to begin with. At 60, I notice a greater difficulty with fine motor control (coordination, not car engines), but I always had difficulties there. I suppose I am seeing changes I would see in later years without Cerebral Palsy. While I am hardly overjoyed with that, I am comfortable with it, and make accommodations in the way I do things.

A lot of my hair is gone and my beard is turning white, but that doesn't bother me either. I look at photos of me from years ago and realize I was much better looking than I ever thought I was back then. So I have never had large amounts of ego tied up in appearance. I find it very sad to see people spend large amounts of effort and focus trying to look younger than they are. Youth should be measured by a sparkle in the eye, not the texture of the skin or the shape of the body.

In my life I have been afraid lots of times, and I am trying to figure out the difference between then and now. I was afraid hanging upside down from a fouled parachute, but it was a clean fear, an immediate fear. The answer is playing tag inside my head, always visible but just out of reach. Or perhaps I am just unwilling to look it in the face.

I remember the arrogance of the young, staring at the North Atlantic in all her fury without fear. I remember the simplicity of childhood, doing what I was told simply because I was told. I remember the seeming security of adulthood, believing I could do whatever needed to be done.

Now it is winter in Illinois. Taking out the trash, I forget to turn on the porch light, and looking at the step down from the porch, I am afraid. Is there ice, will I fall? At least for now, I step anyway, refusing to give into fear. Or perhaps I simply don't care, I am not sure. While not a personal focus, I also have my dark times.

Once in a while, it all comes crashing in. When it does, you just need to hang on and get by. Folks loved and gone. Folks loved and absent. You just grab your bootstraps and hang on. Tears and pain WILL roll off, especially if you're hanging onto your bootstraps. If you are honest, you have hurt people. Everyone does. So get tough, and live with it. And go on, because there is no option.

Crank up the radio and cry. Do not drive, unless there is a winter storm chasing you from Spokane. If there is, drive like a demon! What is already gone cannot be lost. Drive like a demon through the Rockies, like a devil across the plains. Hammer down through it all and get by.

Race the wind and win! The road is a ribbon, and passage is the object. Hug the curves and hammer down on straights, in life as on a road in Montana. You cannot go back, but you can go on. That, I think, is the message here. Hammer down, life is finite and is what we make of it.

Dark times, like storms, can be weathered.

Epilogue

Well, it's late, the radio is playing a patriotic country western song, and half a world away Americans are fighting to guarantee my freedom. I think of that refrain in a song, "what a long strange trip it's been", by the Grateful Dead, I think? It sure has been an interesting trip for me.

A quick thought, if you have skipped to the back of the book, then shame on you! You are probably the kind of person who stirs a chocolate malted!

Be well, be safe, and God bless! Oh, and have fun, too.

John